The Mind's Arrows

The Mind's Arrows

Bayes Nets and Graphical Causal Models in
Psychology

Clark Glymour

A Bradford Book
The MIT Press
Cambridge, Massachusetts
London, England

This book was set in Sabon by Asco Typesetters, Hong Kong, on 3B2 and was printed and bound in the United States of America.

First printing, 2001

Library of Congress Cataloging-in-Publication Data

Glymour, Clark N.
  The mind's arrows : Bayes nets and graphical causal models in psychology / Clark Glymour.
      p.   cm.
  "A Bradford book."
  Includes bibliographical references and index.
  ISBN 0-262-07220-3 (alk. paper)
  1. Psychology—Methodology. 2. Prediction theory. 3. Causation. I. Title.
BF38.5 .G59 2001
150'.1—dc21   2001032623

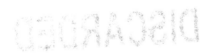

In memory of my teachers Cynthia Ann Schuster and Wesley Charles Salmon

Contents

Acknowledgments

In a way, this book began thirty years ago. While I was at work on a methodological history of psychoanalysis, Leon Kamin gave me the manuscript of his book on intelligence testing, *Science and IQ*. That led me to read more on psychometrics and, increasingly, cognitive psychology. I came to the conclusion that most of the deficiencies in Freud's science are deficiencies as well in contemporary theories of cognitive architecture, whether founded on psychometrics or on now more fashionable techniques in cognitive psychology, and so in a sense my history was unfair to Freud and his followers. I rewrote the manuscript as a historical parallelism with a methodological moral. While I thought its thesis was true (and, sadly, I still do), the result was thoroughly mean, and the unhappy manuscript sat in a cupboard for several years, dragged out now and then for unsatisfactory repairs. In the meanwhile, more productive work concerned the causal interpretation of Bayes nets and computational learning theory. In the 1980s, though conversations with several people, especially Martha Farah and Jeff Bub, I began to think that there were important but unnoticed connections between causal Bayes nets, computational learning theory, and contemporary cognitive psychology. This book is the result. Freud is still in the cupboard.

The methodological ideas in this book are indebted to Kevin Kelly, Dan Osherson, Judea Pearl, Thomas Richardson, Richard Scheines, Peter Spirtes, Gregory Cooper, and Scott Weinstein. My application of these ideas to psychology is indebted to years of conversation with three psychologists—Patricia Cheng, Martha Farah, and Alison Gopnik—and to more recent conversations with Susan Johnson, John Watson, and Joshua Tenenbaum. Chapter 3, in particular, emerged from joint work with Gopnik, and parts of chapter 7 from joint work with Cheng, to whom I am especially grateful for her patient explanations and corrections of my many errors, mathematical and otherwise. Chapter 9 was prompted by discussions with Gopnik and Tenenbaum. In chapter 6, I applied some results of brilliant work on Rescorla and Wagner's model by my brilliant student David Danks. Allen Hobson posed to me the problem addressed in chapter 13. There is a pleasing something—irony? closure?—in the fact that aspects of part II of this book are concerned with the Rescorla-Wagner model of learning, which exploits a suggestion of Kamin's, and aspects of part IV are concerned with inferences from intelligence tests, an issue to which Kamin first introduced me. So, although I have not met or talked with him in twenty five years, there is another debt. Patricia Cheng, David Danks, and, especially, Peter Spirtes corrected many of my errors, probably not enough of them.

Parts of chapter 2 appeared in *Synthese*. A fragment of Chapter 3 appeared in "Bayes Nets as Psychological Models," in the volume *Explanation and Cognition*, edited by Frank Keil and Robert Wilson. Chapter 10 is an elaboration of an essay published in the *British Journal for Philosophy of Science* in 1994. Chapter 13 was written in collaboration with Thomas Richardson and Peter Spirtes and accepted for publication by *Philosophy of Science* some years ago, subject to elaborations we did not want to take the trouble to make, and which are unnecessary in the context of this volume. I thank Richardson and Sprites for permitting me to publish it here. Chapter 14 is an amalgam of two essays on the Bell Curve, one from *Philosophy of Science* and the other from a volume published by Springer-Verlag.

I am obliged to Carnegie Mellon University, to the National Aeronautics and Space Administration and the NASA Ames Research Center, and to the National Science Foundation, the last of which supported work on part III of this book through grant SES-9910931. I have personal debts to Ken Ford, Ted Roush, and Joseph Ramsey. Ford, who worked both at Ames and at the Institute for Human and Machine Cognition at the University of West Florida, subpoenaed my assistance for a project at Ames on autonomous robotic mineral identification, which led to a grant from Ames that enabled Carnegie Mellon to free me from teaching duties for a year. Thanks to Roush, at Ames, and to the heroic efforts of Ramsey, who has been my programmer for the project, the work went very smoothly and fruitfully, and permitted me marginal time over several months to work on this book. Alan Thwaits made the manuscript clearer and more graceful.

To my teachers Cynthia Schuster and Wesley Salmon I owe debts of a lifetime.

Cynthia Schuster and Wesley Salmon studied with Hans Reichenbach at UCLA in the early 1950s. Cynthia and her husband, Philip, came to UCLA after many years in Europe, where, after they had finished their undergraduate study at Cornell hc in literature, she in chemistry—they had gone in the 1930s as young, optimistic American expatriates, only to be caught up in the Second World War and interned in a German camp in France. Wes had come to come to UCLA from undergraduate school in Michigan. The young man and the older knockabout woman became friends, and later both became my teachers.

Cynthia took and lost a job at Washington State University. In the 1950s, in the grip of McCarthyism, the State of Washington had its own Un-Washington Activities Committee (you can read about it in Owen Lattimore's *Ordeal by Slander*). In part because of her invitation to Robert Oppenheimer to speak on campus, Cynthia was charged with undermining the morals of youth (the irony of the charge pleased her no end) and dismissed from her job. She moved to the University of Montana, where she was my teacher for two years, until I was dismissed as a student. Wes first took a temporary position at UCLA (to qualify for it, he wrote his doctoral dissertation in 11 days!), then at Northwestern, Brown, and Indiana, where (as appeared almost equally important in my eyes, but not in his) he married Merrilee Salmon and supervised my doctoral dissertation. Later Wes, Merrilee, and I became colleagues at Pitt, where, for a brief period, Wes was chair of the Philosophy Department and I was chair of the Department of History and Philosophy of Science. Wes and Merrilee gave an unchristening party for the birth of my daughter Holly, and so they are, after a fashion, her godparents.

Cynthia was a woman of stories, for the most part about Europe during the war. Wes was a man of one-liners. Their stories and one-liners tell more about them than do my sentimental memories, and are more fun. I will recount my favorite of Cynthia's many stories and a few of Wes's one-liners.

At the beginning of the war, Cynthia and Phil found themselves living on a farm outside Montpelier. The war cut off their income and food supply, and they made do, not very well, with a garden and an ample supply of seed potatoes. One day Phil collapsed in the garden, and Cynthia knew something had to be done to find them more to eat. The farmer and his family down the road had a similar problem, although the farmer was in better physical condition than Phil. The two families, French and American, were friendly: Cynthia, a chemist, had shown the farmer's wife how to make a loaf of bread rise without the special yeast the French favored but could no longer obtain. Cynthia and the farmer struck a deal. The farmer had a horse and a year's supply of ration cards allotted to him for horse carrots, but he had no seed. Cynthia would give the farmer her seed potatoes; the farmer would get his year's supply of horse carrots all at once and give them to Cynthia and Phil, then kill the horse, share the meat, and render the rest of the horse into soap that could be sold on the black market. The farmer duly delivered the horse carrots to Cynthia and Phil and took away the seed potatoes. The next day Cynthia bicycled over to the neighbors, only to find a disaster. The starving farm cat, gorged on the fat of the drying soap, lay bloated and dead in the yard in front of the farmhouse, broken pieces of gray soap scattered around him, a fortune destroyed. From the stoop where she sat in tears, the farmer's wife looked up at Cynthia, dismounting from her bicycle, and asked, "Madame, les chimistes Americains, comment font-ils se parer la chatte et le savon?"

When qualifying examinations approached at Indiana, I suddenly developed signs of serious diseases—heart trouble, quite possibly cancer. My file at the student health center, where I stopped each morning on my way to classes, became the thickest on record. Finally, a few days before the scheduled exam, the physician gave me a letter excusing me on grounds of health, which I happily presented to Wes, who excused me from the exam. What else could he do? With freedom from the qualifying exam, my symptoms vanished as mysteriously as they had come. I was well, although my academic career was not. One afternoon, two weeks later, at ease with the world, I was walking down a corridor when Wes pulled me into his office and spoke one sentence to me. I would take the qualifying examination the next morning, he said (not "asked"). I did, and I passed.

I wrote my master's thesis, which Wes supervised, on identity through time. At my oral thesis examination, with the bound document on the table before them, the other examiners asked various technical questions of no particular interest, but Wes said nothing, until, near the end, he asked one question: "Can you prove to me this is the same thesis I read?"

When, two years later, I passed my doctoral oral, Wes shook my hand and gave me a piece of advice I should have better heeded before undertaking this book: "Remember, Clark," he said, "if you publish nothing, you're even."

The Mind's Arrows

1

Introduction

In several senses, causal relations are, or ought to be, the subjects of cognitive psychology. Virtually all of the divisions of cognitive psychology (and related subjects, psychometrics for example) are about the causal processes and mechanisms through which intelligent action comes about. Subdisciplines—human adult judgement and developmental psychology, for examples—are chiefly about the processes and mechanisms through which human understanding of causal relations comes about, the causes of our knowledge of the causal structure of the world. Other than by luck, cognitive science will succeed only if scientific inferences to causes are made by reliable procedures. And adequate theories of human understanding require knowing what it is that people have when they have causal knowledge, and how they come to have it. These tangled issues are the subjects of this book.

In the last decade, small groups of statisticians, computer scientists, and philosophers have developed a theory about how to represent causal relations and how causal claims connect with probabilities. From those representations there follow accounts of how information about some features of the world may be used to compute probabilities for other features, accounts of how partial causal knowledge may be used to compute the effects of actions, and accounts of how causal relations can be reliably learned, at least by computers. The objects of the theory are sometimes called causal Bayes nets, sometimes referred to by a more general category, graphical causal models. The differences are technical. Briefly, graphical causal models include structures with feedback, but Bayes nets do not.

Causal Bayes nets, and graphical causal models more generally, are surely an incomplete representation of the variety and wealth of causal constructions we use in science and everyday life, but they apply widely enough, I claim, to be surprisingly useful in psychological theory, in the interpretation of psychological experiments, and in guiding and evaluating causal inferences in psychology. More than useful, essential. This book consists of illustrations of this thesis in studies of adult judgement, in developmental psychology, in cognitive neuropsychology, and in psychometrics and social psychology. The illustrations are both positive and negative. I suggest that theories—the *theory theory*—of how cognition develops in infants and children can be fruitfully elaborated by supposing that one of the main tasks of children is to learn the causal structure of the world, and that what is to be learned, and how it could possibly be learned, is illuminated by causal Bayes nets. I show, or at least claim to show, that the results of well-known experiments in adult judgement have been seriously misinterpreted, and that well-known theories of adult causal judgement entail a range of unrecognized, and so untested (but testable), predictions. These suggestions lead to proposals for psychological experiments that have not been done and interesting projects in the development of heuristic learning procedures, including the formation of categories. They include a sketch of an approach to the frame problem, which I understand as the task of specifying feasible algorithmic procedures by which factors relevant to actions and plans can be isolated from irrelevant factors.

In cognitive neuropsychology, so-called "box and arrow diagrams" are causal hypotheses, in fact graphical causal models with extremal (that is, 0 or 1) probabilities. Using the graphical representation and elementary computational learning theory, I investigate two methodological questions that have been disputed at length in the neuropsychological literature: What inferences can be reliably made from the study of the deficits of brain damaged individuals? What inferences can be reliably made if such data are aggregated in various ways to yield "group data"? Bayes nets are a species of neural nets, which are in turn a species of graphical causal models. Reintroducing probabilities, I use graphical causal models to begin to address arguments in cognitive neuropsychology based on the behavior of lesioned neural networks representing brain damage. Can any mathematically possible combination of normal and brain-damaged behaviors be explained by postulating some neural network representing the normal brain (or normal functional architecture) and lesioning it appropriately?

Many of the statistical models used in psychometrics and in social psychology are graphical causal models in disguise. That recognition, combined with what we know about inference to graphical causal models from data, ought, I argue, to change radically the technology that social psychologists use to represent causal hypotheses, and the methods by which they argue for them. There is a dismaying unity between social statistics and psychological interpretations of adult judgements of causation. The fallacies of statistical methods popular in social statistics—regression and factor analysis—become, in the experiments of some cognitive psychologists, the norms against which the judgements of experimental subjects are assessed. Subjects make judgements that are sometimes, perhaps often, normatively correct, and on the basis of those judgements, psychologists, or some of them, claim to have discovered features of human irrationality so fundamental that, were these psychologists correct, our capacity to get around in the world would become quite mysterious. A central fallacy in regression is the very same error that occurs in many psychological interpretations of experiments on adult human judgement, the topic of much of part 2 of this book. All that changes from cognitive psychology to social psychology is the mathematical clothing of the fallacy. Psychologists are the victims in this practice, the victims of confusions about causal inference buried in the statistical methods they have borrowed from other disciplines. I hope to persuade them that there are better lenders. The points are illustrated with a discussion of the use of data and causal hypotheses in *The Bell Curve*, surely the most notorious work of social science in the last decade, but they equally apply to many less famous efforts in social psychology.

Two features of this book require brief apology. First, while many experiments are proposed, and many are analyzed, this book contains no details of any original experiments. My scientific training is in chemistry and chemical physics, not psychology, and I was never very good even in the chemistry laboratory. I have the greatest admiration for the ingenuity and wealth of tacit knowledge that enables good psychological experimenters to get clean results. Second, psychological papers on causal judgement often begin with reviews of philosophical metaphysics about causation, generally citing Hume and Kant. There is none of that here, and in the usual sense of the moderns, but not of the ancients, there is no philosophy. I do not propose a philosophical *analysis* of causation, and except as they present experimental ambiguities, I am not much concerned with how people express themselves when making causal judgements or when offering causal explanations. My concern in developmental psychology, for example, is less with how children come to generate explicit causal explanations and more with how they come to be able to predict and control their environment. Even so, a number of distinctions about kinds of causal knowledge necessarily emerge in the discussion.

So far as possible, I have suppressed formalism and mathematical details. Undoubtedly, many readers will think not nearly enough. While I have provided a brief summary of causal Bayes nets and their properties in chapter 3, for the most part I have tried to motivate the essential ideas through examples from the psychological literature. Especially in parts III and IV, substantive discussion is interrupted by historical digressions. I believe that historical considerations are an essential tool for understanding the fundamental problems that motivated the introduction of technical methods and for seeing how contemporary techniques have either solved or evaded those problems. I also think that historical perspective sometimes diminishes the sense of contemporary originality, and rightly so.

I

Developmental Psychology and Discovery

2

Android Epistemology for Babies

2.1 Introduction

At its birth in nineteenth century neuropsychology, the most successful strategy of cognitive psychology was decomposition. Apparently indivisible intelligent capacities were shown to consist of a complex of less intelligent component subcapacities. When parts of our machinery are broken—when our brains are damaged—we behave irrationally or incompetently, and our failings reveal something of the brain's mechanisms. The psychologists of the day allowed that, when whole, we are still the grand, rational creatures we had taken ourselves to be since the Enlightenment. Freud, who began his professional career as a neuropsychologist, extended the strategy to psychological breakage, but he and his disciples gave a post-Enlightenment twist to abnormal behavior and rationality.

By the middle of the twentieth century, a certain pessimistic parallelism emerged in social and cognitive psychology. Through a series of slightly shocking experiments, social psychologists argued that features of character we think are stable are really artifacts of context. Change the context sufficiently and the kind become vile, the brave become servile, the gentle become cruel. At about the same time, Paul Meehl (perhaps not accidentally, a psychoanalyst) argued that simple algorithms make better predictions than do expert clinical psychologists. Meehl and his contemporaries in social psychology anticipated a genre that is now standard in cognitive psychology. Cognitive or ethical behavior is compared with some normative standard, and humans are found wanting. Well-designed machines would optimize; we are machines that can only satisfice, on a good day. According to received opinion in cognitive psychology, we are ill-constructed, incompetent machines, without firm character, unable to act by moral or rational standards, deluded that our conscious deliberations cause (at least some of) our actions. The one bit of intelligence left us, science, is an unstable oddity that we sustain only through elaborate social mechanisms.

We might have guessed most of this from the newspapers, or any reading of history. Still, we are smarter than toasters and thermostats. We are a lot smarter than any machine we have been able to build. Even children who grow up to be fundamentalists and postmodernists learn a natural language, everyday physics, spatiotemporal regularities, commonsense psychology, and a wealth of causal relations involving people and things. Whatever our ambitions for artificial intelligence, no machine as yet comes close. The most intelligent things about us are not what we do or what we know, but that we have learned to do or to know. The common complaint that Turing's famous test for intelligence set too high a standard for machine intelligence has got it upside down: for intelligence like ours, a computer should not only be able to hold a conversation that imitates a man's, or imitates a man imitating a woman, it should be able to learn to hold such a conversation, in any natural language, from the data available to any child in the environment of that language. Turing thought as much himself.[1] For machines we can build, that would be a dream, if only machines we can build could dream. If we're so dumb, how come we're so smart?

2.2   Children

In 1998 my six-year-old daughter, Madelyn Rose, had a frog named James. James and Madelyn had rather different worlds. Judged by his behavior, James's world was pretty well described by a language with just two predicates: "brown-spot-in-water" and "fast-large-motion-nearby." When James was a tadpole, his world may have been simpler, but it can't have been a lot simpler. Madelyn's amazing world was filled with things with various powers, all of which she knew about and knew how to use; people, with mental states she matched or contrasted with her own; complex relationships of indescribably many kinds; and a language she could speak and read and sort of write and tell bad jokes in.[2] She had explanations for her world, pretty good explanations even when off the mark.[3] When she was born, to all appearances she knew none of this. How did she come to be such a know-it-all?

What we seem to know from developmental psychology is this: Madelyn was born able to discriminate up-close objects, with the ability to judge whether there were one or several such objects and with a disposition to reidentify objects that moved continuously in her field of view. She also identified the objects of one sense with the objects of another—the same object was seen and touched. By the age at which she could control her head a bit, she could reidentify objects that had not moved when she had turned her head so that they were out of her field of vision and then turned it back. By six months she could reidentify objects by predicting a trajectory when they had been out of her sight for part of that trajectory, as long as the total trajectory was very simple, e.g., a straight line. She made lots of mistakes—in particular, she thought things that disappear tend to be where they were last seen, even in contexts where that was repeatedly falsified. At about nine months she began to think that people in different positions see different aspects of an object, the details of which she was still working out at 18 months. By 12 months, using constancy or near constancy of perceptual features, she could reidentify objects that had been out of sight for a while, and she largely overcame the mistake of thinking things remained where last seen, although she could still be fooled. By 18 months she was reidentifying objects from perception more or less like an adult, but her understanding of what others perceive was still not correct. By age 3 she had got right others' perceptions of objects—at least what is visible and what is invisible to whom.

Madelyn was born knowing how to imitate some facial expressions. Within a couple of months she had learned that certain of her actions, in certain contexts, produced a result, and that in some cases the result varied with the intensity of the action (as in kicking). She tended for a long while to radically overgeneralize and undergeneralize connections between her actions and their consequences. If pulling a blanket with a toy on it brought the toy to her, she would pull the blanket even when the toy was beside, not on, the blanket.

In this same period Madelyn learned to crawl and to walk, and she began to learn to talk. According to psychologists, the timing of these skills was not accidental. Crawling improves judgements about reidentification (or "object permanence"), and judgements about objects that are out of sight develop at about the time that a general word for absence ("gone") enters speech.

Madelyn's psychological knowledge went through a similar series of stages. For a while she did not recognize that others' beliefs, or her own, could be false. Her judgements of what was believed were a subset of her judgements of what was true. Eventually she came round to our distinctions.

At six, and even before, her knowledge of folk psychology and folk physics and spoken English were essentially complete. She still had some odd false beliefs (she thought she spoke Spanish because she spent her first year in Costa Rica), but then don't we all?

2.3   The Platonic Theory of Cognitive Development

Developmental psychology has been mostly an account of stages. At certain ages infants do this, then that, later something else. As with butterflies from caterpillars, going through stages, even amazing stages, even stages that lead to the right answer, may make a thing or person interesting, but not smart. Compare a developmental version of Kevin Kelly's Einstein machine:[4] the first hundred data points you put in, it responds with $E = mc$; the next hundred $E = mc^3$; after that $E = mc^2$. It does nothing else. In this world, the Einstein machine converges to the right answer; in any conceivable world in which the energy equation is different in any way, the Einstein machine gets the wrong answer or no answer at all. By increasing or slowing the rate at which data are input, you can change how soon the Einstein machine converges to Einstein's equation; by stopping the data input before 201 data points are submitted, you can stunt its growth. But that's about all you can do. Nothing could be more different than the Einstein machine and Einstein, at least the popular Einstein: the popular Einstein would have found the truth whatever it might have been (as long as it was beautiful, simple, etc.), and he found a lot of other truths besides the energy equation. The popular Einstein was smart; the Einstein machine is stupid. (But from another viewpoint, the two, Einstein and the Einstein machine, differ only in degree, only in the range of different possible circumstances in which they find differing truths.)

Some psychologists think kids—and therefore all of us—are Einstein machines. We will, given normal stimulation, develop the right cognitive skills and beliefs for this, our actual environment, no matter what else; speeding up the stimulation may speed up the development timing, and slowing the stimulation may slow it down. Abnormal stimulation in place of normal stimulation just stops development. Put in a world where objects can pass, or appear to pass, through other objects, where people have visual perception out of their line of sight, where objects really vanish when out of perception and don't reappear, where an unhuman language is spoken, children could not adapt their beliefs and skills accordingly. What goes on in development is like data decompression triggered by outside events, just as Plato claimed in *The Meno* 2,500 years ago. Sometimes this is called the *modular* view of development, which doesn't seem very descriptive.

The modular view of development can be traced to Plato, but there are twentieth-century philosophical sources as well. Rudolf Carnap, Bertrand Russell, and C. I. Lewis had similar philosophical educations, first in the conventional turn-of-the-century neo-Kantianism, second in mathematical logic. Russell proposed a combination of the two in *Our Knowledge of the External World*. The world delivers to us the matter of sensation (Kant's term) or sense data (Russell's term) or qualia (Lewis's term). We (unconsciously, presumably) supply the apparatus of logic and an elaborate scheme of definitions, which, when applied to the particulars of sense data, (literally) *define* objects, processes, space, time, and relations of all kinds. The world we experience just *is* logical combinations of sense data. Russell doesn't work out much of the details. C. I. Lewis gave a very similar story in *Mind and the World Order*, again without the details. Carnap was a detail guy. *Der Logische Aufbau der Welt* assumes that what is given in sensation is a gestalt, an entire experience at a moment, not particulate sense data that have to be assembled into a gestalt. What is given in reflection, according to Carnap, is the recollection that two gestalts are in some respect similar. With these primitives, Carnap offered explicit logical schemes to represent sensory modalities, objects, space, and time. What's more, he realized (in 1928!) that he was writing a program, and in parallel with the definitions, he offered "fictional procedures" to construct an instantiation of whatever entity he was defining. Carnap's logical effort was revived in the 1940s by Nelson Goodman in *The Structure of Appearance*, which explored various logical methods of definition and various constructions from different primitive bases. Carnap's hints about procedures were not followed up.

Several things strike me as interesting about this bit of philosophical history, now regarded by most philosophers who know of it as so much logical weirdness. First, it was equivocally substantive psychological theory; Russell and Lewis claimed to be giving an account of how the mind works. Carnap, who actually did some ingenious mathematical work, muddled issues by claiming he was giving a "reconstruction" and a "logical justification" of something, although of just what is unclear. Carnap never wrote the plain and obvious thing, that his theory aimed to be an idealized, and therefore approximate, account of how we think. Although his work was arguably the most ambitious mathematical psychology of the time, psychologists then took (and now take) no notice of it. Second, none of this work is about how our judgements of the world come to be reliably correct. The view of Russell, Lewis, Carnap, and Goodman is not that there is a world out there of things and properties and processes and minds and relationships, veridical representations of which we are constituted to construct. The world *is* what we construct from primitive inputs. We can be wrong in our expectations of future inputs, but not about any thing else empirical.

It requires only a turn of perspective to see these philosophical efforts as attempts to describe a modular mind, a system of Einstein machines, of the kind many contemporary cognitive psychologists seem to think we are. And contemporary philosophy still finds the modular view of development remarkably congenial. According to Jerry Fodor (1983), for all but the highest-order processing, modules are the end state of development, and these views seem to be shared by a number of philosophers.

Artificial intelligence is equally friendly to the modular viewpoint, at least partly because it is difficult enough to give a computational account of relatively developed, distinct skills, let alone a theory of how such skills could be acquired. Naive physics, the artificial intelligence theory of how a robot might compute the ordinary behavior of everyday solids and liquids, is an interesting descendant of the efforts of Russell, Lewis, Carnap, and Goodman, and it bears on the Einstein-machine view of development. The idea is to formalize (preferably in a computationally tractable way) the principles of everyday commonsense adult knowledge of the identity and behavior of middle-sized dry and wet goods. That must include principles about containment, occlusion, disappearance and reappearance, comovement of parts or regions, identity through time and through changes of properties, causal interactions that influence shape and motion, and so on—all topics investigated in developmental psychology. So far as I know, those working on naive physics have paid little attention to developmental psychology (with rare exceptions, the inattention is mutual), but the naive physics project, if brought to fruition, would imply a procedural characterization of adult (and six-year-old) competencies.

2.4 The Theory Theory

The views Alison Gopnik and Andrew Meltzoff offer in *Words, Thoughts, and Theories* are, so far as I know, the principal development in psychology that offers an Enlightenment picture of human capacities.[5] They say that children are more like the popular Einstein than they are like Einstein machines. What Gopnik and Meltzoff think Madelyn Rose did as she grew from zero to six was this: she did science. She formed theories, made observations, conducted experiments, formed empirical generalizations, revised her theories, altered her "conceptual scheme," explained things, collected or ignored anomalies. Within limits, had she lived in a world with a different everyday physics (say, for example, she grew up without gravity, the Virginia Dare of space stations), she would have developed a different, but correct, theory of the physics of everyday things. If she had grown up in 'toon land, where even the concrete can talk and buckle and have eyes bug out, she would have had a different theory of kinds, attooned to her environment. Children are scientists, in fact the ideal scientists imagined in old-fashioned philosophy of science, with a desire for understanding and control of the environment, unbiased by competition, without need for tenure, with deference to elder scientists when they can be understood, with an abundance of data available, with endless leisure. Their inquiry may be unconscious, or only partly conscious, but so is the thinking of individual adult scientists.

　　Here is a Rousseauian theory of cognitive development that rides on philosophy of science, more or less as philosophers in the fifties and sixties understood science, a theory that offers a radically rational view of each of us at our beginning. Man is born brilliant but is almost everywhere stupid. If ordinary adults have a huge irrational streak (committed to absurd gods, alien abductions, and creationism), it is because, unlike children, they deal with issues for which there is a paucity of evidence, or because social forces corrupt their native rationality.[6]

2.5   Android Epistemology

If we are not Einstein machines, we may still be machines of a more adaptive, more ingenious, more intelligent kind. Most philosophers in the twentieth century believed that, even with social complexities aside, the process of inquiry could not be algorithmic, or as they put it, there is no logic of discovery. As machine learning has advanced in the last decades and automated methods have seeped into many sciences, these philosophical cavils have become increasingly quaint. Android epistemology is the still-nascent study of how computational systems could, starting with various primitive abilities and sensory inputs, come to know about their world. Carnap was its unwitting founder.

The theory theory embraces an optimistic reliabilism: within limits, children will converge to the truth, whatever the truth may be. The project of baby android epistemology helps make sense of the theory theorists' reliabilism. Convergence of belief and behavior is what one would expect if baby scientific theorizing isn't a free creation, but is the application of algorithms that (as theory theorists suggest) start with an initial theory and have rules for elaborating, retracting, or revising theory in the light of data, for acquiring new data, and for attending to some of the data while neglecting other parts, and that have metarules for revising rules. If the data are sufficiently overwhelming with respect to the theoretical options available to the baby, then the algorithms need not even be deterministic or entirely invariant from individual to individual.

Reliable convergence is one thing, reliable convergence to the *truth* another. According to the philosophers (from Plato to Popper and after), there cannot be an algorithm that uses only singular data (no quantified data) and that has the following properties: in all conceivable worlds in which a universal proposition is true, the algorithm converges to asserting the proposition, and in all worlds in which it is false, the algorithm converges to asserting its denial. The claim is in developmental psychology's philosophical source, *The Meno*; the proof is in the writing of the fourth-century skeptic, Sextus Empiricus. To the ancient argument, contemporary philosophers of science have added only anecdote: even the best confirmed and accepted scientific theories often turn out to be false; witness Newton's. But the proof, and the relevance of the anecdotes, depend on an unnecessarily stringent criterion of success in inquiry. The philosophers require that the algorithm be equivalent to a procedure that, after receiving some finite array of evidence, gives a single conjecture, and in every possible world gives the conjecture that is correct in that world.

There are two dimensions of alternative success criteria: the kind of convergence required for success, and the range of circumstances for which success is required. An algorithm for learning need not give the truth and only the truth in each possible world; we might require, for example, only that in each possible world there comes a time after which the algorithm ceases making erroneous conjectures and ever after conjectures the truth,[7] or we might require any of a hierarchy of still weaker criteria. An algorithm for learning need not succeed in all possible worlds, but only in a large and interesting set of possible worlds (the theory theorists do not assert that babies would learn the essentials in every consistent world in which they survived; they claim there is an ill-characterized range of worlds in which babies would do so). Weakening the success criteria in either dimension strengthens the logical content of learnable hypotheses.[8] The less that is demanded for success, the more success there will be.

There is more. Theory theorists claim that babies undergo internal conceptual revolutions; whole groups of theoretical notions dominant at one stage of development are abandoned and replaced by others at later stages of development. At every stage the categorizations that evolve seem to have an element of artifice; they are conceptual schemes about the mental and physical into which particular events are fitted and shoved. In C. I. Lewis's terminology, the babies evolve different "pragmatic a priori" conceptions; in Carnap's, they evolve different languages; in Thomas Kuhn's, different "paradigms." For the philosophical tradition, "conceptual revolution" carries a burden of which the theory theorists take no notice: conceptual changes alter the meanings of words and sentences and change truth values. ("Up" and "down" meant different things to Aristotelians and to Newtonians, for example.) Right or wrong (I think wrong), the philosophers' picture of conceptual change, more or less explicit from early in the twentieth century until now, is that truth is fixed by the world and the conceptual scheme together. Surely, there can't be any notion of an algorithm reliably converging to the truth if the very output of the algorithm changes what is true.

Yes there can. Actually, several interesting notions. For example, the learning algorithm can eventually converge to a single conceptual scheme within which it converges to the truth, or the learning algorithm can vacillate among conceptual schemes, within each of which it converges to the truth. There is a well-worked-out abstract theory of relativistic convergence to the truth, and there are characterizations of algorithms that converge to the (relative) truth. Even radical social relativism, in which the beliefs of the community determine the truth, admits a reliability analysis.[9]

Theory theorists, steeped in the computational conception of mind, suggest that infants and children embody algorithms for inquiry that in normal circumstances lead them to converge not just on the truth about the world but also on the *capacity* quickly to know the truth over a range of circumstances. But the theory theorists give no hints about the content of learning algorithms or how they can reliably succeed. While the data on stages of development may not determine a unique algorithm of inquiry, perhaps it can sufficiently constrain algorithms to make a computational theory of development an interesting project. The project seems to me right at the logical center of the most ambitious aspect of artificial intelligence, android epistemology.

2.6   Issues

Part of what a child acquires within four or five years is knowledge of how to control, prevent, bring about, and predict events and circumstances. Most of that knowledge can be described as of causal relations.

How can a child acquire knowledge of causal relations, starting from the capacity to recognize instances of a number of properties and using data from observation of her own actions, others' actions, and sequences of events without animate causes? Given an initial set of properties, how can a child identify and select other properties that may enter into causal relations? How can the child use acquired causal knowledge for prediction and control in particular circumstances? There is no reason to believe that the first two questions are entirely separable. Learning causal relations depends on identifying appropriate variables; finding appropriate variables may depend on what causal relations are already known and on what causal relations can be learned with what variables.

The psychological literature about concept formation is considerable, but psychologists have not been so kind to questions about learning causal relations. Piaget gave accounts of children's causal beliefs, but said comparatively little about how they are arrived at. Pavlov and Skinner avoided talk of learning causes in favor of learning associations, although the salient difference between classical and operant conditioning is that the former teaches associations while the latter teaches a limited kind of causal connection. The neural-network model, which is hidden beneath a lot of twentieth-century psychology, from Freud to Thorndike and after, promoted the study of associations. Many recent psychological models of causal inference are derived from a neural-network model (Rescorla and Wagner's model) and explicitly confound learning associations with learning causes. And many psychologists hold that the notion of a mechanism is essential to separating causes from other features of a situation and deny that there is any algorithmic basis for using patterns of association to separate causes from other factors.

Artificial intelligence provides no ready answer to these issues. But there is a computational representation of causal knowledge—causal Bayes nets—and there is a developed theory of how those networks can be discovered from observations and experiments and of how they can be used in prediction and planning. The following chapter develops a sketchy proposal for how the theory of Bayes-net representations, discovery algorithms, and prediction algorithms might be elaborated and modified to bear on the issues of human cognitive development.

3

Another Way for Nerds to Make Babies: The Frame Problem and Causal Inference in Developmental Psychology

3.1 The Frame Problem

Artificial intelligence and developmental psychology share areas of genuine common interest, and most of them have to do with a cluster of issues called the "frame problem." The frame problem began as an interesting technical curiosity. In discussing logical descriptions of world states (or partial world states, "situations"), McCarthy and Hayes (1969) considered how to formalize changes in the state of the world, for example, those resulting from actions. The problem, as they viewed it, was how to specify the entire state consequent from an action in terms of the prior state, a formal description of the action or event, and axioms about change. To do so, they found themselves forced to introduce an enormous list of trivial "frame axioms" specifying not only what changes but also everything that *does not* change under an action. The problem, initially, was to find a formal way to dispense with such axioms. Their frame problem was naturally transposed into a problem about planning: how can an automated system, a robot, which has a great deal of knowledge about the state of the world, feasibly predict the consequences of an action it contemplates? Clearly, not by considering every feature of the world it knows about, deciding one by one which of them will be altered by the action and which will not. Drew McDermott (1987) argued that the problem is solved by a single general rule of thumb: other things equal, things not directly changed by an action do not change. Sleeping dogs sleep. Rather than putting the problem to rest, however, McDermott's suggestion implicated a host of issues.

The sleeping-dog rule is an example of default reasoning. For a robot to function successfully in the world using the rule, it must have a means for recovering—for appropriately altering its beliefs about the world when the default rule fails, when sleeping dogs wake up. There follows an enormous and interesting literature on feasible reasoning with defaults. I will not try to review the issues, but some examples may illustrate the richness. Suppose that the robot learns a new fact, observes a change. Then to stay calibrated to the world as it is, the robot's beliefs must be altered in response, since some of the robot's beliefs may be contradicted by the new fact in conjunction with the remainder of its beliefs. How are the revisions to be made? When, for example, a belief is abandoned, are other beliefs that were originally adopted only because of the now abandoned belief also to be abandoned? If not, what is to be done, and if so, how is the robot to keep track? In artificial intelligence this is called the problem of "truth maintenance," or "reason maintenance."

Even if the robot is given norms for revision, how is it feasibly to carry them out? The robot cannot feasibly consider each of its beliefs, one by one, including the consequences of everything it believes, and decide whether the new information is relevant and then make the appropriate revision, if any. Or consider a more mundane problem: how is the robot feasibly to determine the changes that *do* result from the present state of things, with or without actions? How is it to determine, for example, the trajectories of solid objects, or the behavior of liquids when their containers are moved or removed? Surely, the robot cannot feasibly determine where a ball will land by observing a sequence of positions, taking them as initial conditions for a differential equation, and integrating. No one has ever built a robot that can play first base. These are the problems—or some of them—of naive physics.

Fodor (1987) posed another problem for the sleeping-dog rule: whether it is true depends on the properties the robot ascribes to the world. If I turn my refrigerator on, this has no bearing on most of the particles in the universe. But consider this property of particles: being a particle and my refrigerator is turned on. Turning on my refrigerator alters this feature of every particle in the universe. So if the robot starts with concepts of particle and the state of its refrigerator and forms the new concept of fridgeon, the sleeping-dog rule will fail dramatically. Michael Dunn (1990) pointed out that in a logical system developed by Anderson and Belnap, relevance logic, predicates such as Fodor's "fridgeon" cannot be properly defined from "particle" and "refrigerator on." One could reply on Fodor's behalf that many legitimate and important predicates appear to be conjunctions that violate the predicate-formation restrictions of relevance logic, or that all concepts are equal: "fridgeon" does not have to be generated by definition from "particle" and "refrigerator on" even though it is coextensive with their conjunction. How is the robot to know which concepts to use?

The robot's frame problems are also the infant's, the baby's, the toddler's, the child's, and developmental psychology might fruitfully be viewed as the experimental study of how those problems are solved. Since they, any more than robots, cannot perform computational and epistemic miracles, how do infants and children come to form the concepts and have the knowledge that enables them to predict and control their environment? I want to explore the thought that they do part of it by learning what we adults can describe as acquiring, elaborating, and revising causal Bayes nets, and by forming concepts that can be represented as features of those networks. That thought leads to natural interpretations of a few experiments with infants and young children, and to suggestions of a variety of experiments that have not been performed. Before considering the few relevant experiments in developmental psychology, consider how causal relations, as represented by Bayes nets, can be learned and how new concepts within, or about, such networks can be introduced. (For a more technical discussion, see Boutelier and Goldzmidt 1996).

3.2 A Toy Introduction to the Markov Assumption

A child acquires information about what happens when she does nothing but observe events, and about what happens when she takes particular kinds of actions, and about what happens when others take particular kinds of actions. She may do one thing and observe a chain of consequences. She may pull a blanket and find that two toys move with it; she may pull the engine in a toy train and find that the tender and the caboose come along; she may pull an electric cord and find that the light and the television go off; she may clap loudly at Grandmother's house and find that the TV and the light come on; she may scream at night and find that the light goes on and a parent appears.

Table 3.1
Experiments at Grandmother's house

Interventions	TV	Light
None	Off	Off
Clap	On	On
Don't clap, turn light switch on	Off	On
Don't clap, turn TV switch on	On	Off
Clap, turn TV switch off	Off	On
Clap, turn light switch off	On	Off

Consider some experiments one might do at Grandmother's house (see table 3.1). In sufficient ignorance one might wonder whether the clapping causes the TV and light to come on by independent mechanisms, or the clapping causes the TV to come on which causes the light to come on, or the clapping causes the light to come on which causes the TV to come on. The experiments establish the first account: Clapping and then turning off the light leaves the TV on. Clapping and then turning off the TV leaves the light on. If the TV is off, turning the light on without clapping does not turn the TV on, and if the light is off, turning the TV on without clapping does not turn the light on. In practical matters, this is the important content of the claim that clapping causes the TV and light to come on by different mechanisms.

The same inferences could be made without intervening to turn the TV on or off or to turn the light on or off, separately from clapping. With some provisos, it suffices to observe that conditional on whether or not a clapping has occurred, the state of the TV and the state of the light are independent (in frequency) of one another. That is, for example, if a clapping occurs, the probability that the TV is on and the light is on equals the product of the probability that the TV is on and the probability that the light is on. The provisos are that the TV does not always respond to the clapping and the light does not always respond to the clapping (sometimes the TV is unplugged, sometimes the light bulb is burnt out). Here is the principle:

Principle 1   If A, B, C are associated, and A is prior to B and C, and A, B, C are not deterministically related, B and C are independent (in probability) given A, and there are no common causes of A and B or of

Table 3.2
Experiments with a toy train

Intervention	State of motion		
None	Engine at rest	Tender at rest	Caboose at rest
Pull engine	Engine moves	Tender moves	Caboose moves
Disconnect tender from engine and pull tender	Engine at rest	Tender moves	Caboose moves
Disconnect tender from engine and pull engine	Engine moves	Tender at rest	Caboose at rest
Disconnect tender from caboose and pull engine	Engine moves	Tender moves	Caboose at rest

A and *C*, then, ceteris paribus, *A* influences *B* and *C* through separate mechanisms.

I will elaborate on the ceteris paribus conditions later.

Consider a different example, the toy train, that illustrates a further connection between probabilistic independence and causality. And, for the purpose of illustration, ignore the causal information that the spatial arrangement of engine, tender, and caboose may give. In each case, we start with the engine, tender, and caboose linked together in order. Table 3.2 gives the results of some experiments one might do.

If the engine is pulled (without directly pulling the caboose), the state of motion of the engine is independent of the state of motion of the caboose, given the state of motion of the tender. In practical terms, that is what it means to say that the motion of the engine influences the motion of the caboose only through the motion of the tender.

Here's the interesting thing. If the couplings between cars were unstable (as they always were with my toy trains), so that the cars sometimes separated of themselves when the engine was pulled, the same inferences to causal structure could be made without ever intervening to uncouple the tender. If only the engine is directly pulled, the motion of the caboose is independent of the motion of the engine given the motion of the tender. The principle is this:

Principle 2 If states of *A*, *B*, *C* are all associated, and the state of *A* is independent (in probability) of the state of *C* given the state of *B*, then, ceteris paribus, the state of *A* influences the state of *C*, if at all, only through the state of *B*.

Causal structures in everyday life manifest themselves by dependencies and independencies upon various interventions or actions, but these causal structures can also manifest themselves by dependencies and independencies without interventions, or with a limited set of interventions.

Different structures may result in different patterns of dependence and independence, and so inferences about causation—about what would happen if an intervention or action were taken—can sometimes be made from data in which no such intervention occurs. Without intervening to keep the tender from moving, it can be determined that if someone were to keep it from moving, the motion of the engine would not influence the motion of the caboose.

3.3   The Causal Markov Assumption

The connections between causal structure and independence or conditional independence illustrated in principles 1 and 2 have a more general formulation, which is almost standard in computer science nowadays and increasingly common in statistics. The formalism, developed over the last twenty years, is used as a method for data analysis in the sciences and engineering, not as a psychological model at all, although its psychological roots are evident in one of its sources: the elicitation from human experts of probabilities to be used in computerized expert systems. The formalism is part of a general representation of causal claims; that representation permits algorithms for inferring aspects of causal structure from appropriate experimental or observational data. The representations are often called "Bayes nets," or sometimes "directed graphical causal models." For causal features that are linearly related, the representations are isomorphic to a subclass of the structures variously called "path models" or "structural equation models." The latter are familiar to some psychologists in the form of "LISREL models," but their causal significance, their isomorphism to Bayes nets, and the existence of sound search algorithms superior to those in standard statistical packages, seem to be unfamiliar. (For details on the connections, see Spirtes et al. 1993, 2001 and Pearl 2000.)

Here is the idea. A possible causal structure will be represented by a directed graph—an object with nodes (hereafter "vertices") and arrows between some of the them. The vertices will represent features or variables, and a directed edge between two variables, $X \rightarrow Y$, will mean that for some values of all of the other variables represented, an action that varies X will cause variation in Y. So the representation of grandmother's appliances would be this:

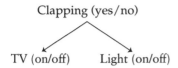

Clapping (yes/no)

TV (on/off)   Light (on/off)

And the representation of causal connections of the toy train when only the engine is pulled would be this:

Engine ⟶ Tender ⟶ Caboose
(moving/not)   (moving/not)   (moving/not)

Factors that do not vary in the data under study are not represented. So, for example, if the electric power is always on, it has no corresponding vertex in the representation for Grandmother's appliance system. If the power supply did vary, the representation would instead be the following:

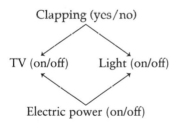

Clapping (yes/no)

TV (on/off)   Light (on/off)

Electric power (on/off)

Suppose that the power supply did vary in the cases at Grandmother's house. Then the associations among clapping, TV state, and light state would not be fully explained by the causal relations of these variables with one another, because a *common cause* of TV state and light state would have been omitted. If no common causes are omitted from a set of variables, the set is said to be *causally sufficient*.

The graph must be acyclic—that is, there is no connected sequence of arrows in the same direction that enters and exits the same vertex.

Therefore, necessarily, in every graph, some of the vertices have no edges directed into them. A vertex with no edge directed into it is said to have *zero indegree* (in graph-theoretic terms), to be *exogenous* (in econometric terms), or to be an *independent variable* (in psychological terms). (To avoid confusion with probabilistic independence, I'll say "exogenous" or "zero indegree.")

The structure of the directed graph encodes probabilistic independence and conditional independence relations among the variables, relations that are claimed to hold in *every* probability distribution that can be generated by varying the exogenous variables independently (in the probabilistic sense). The connection assumed between the causal structure represented by the directed graph, on the one hand, and probabilistic independence and conditional independence, on the other, is given by the Causal Markov Assumption, which says (with boldface for *sets* of variables or nodes):

Causal Markov Assumption   Let X be any variable in a causally sufficient set **S** of variables or features whose causal relations are represented by a directed acyclic graph G, and let **P** be the set of all variables in **S** that are direct causes of X (i.e., parents of X in G). Let **Y** be any subset of **S** such that no variable in **Y** is a direct or indirect effect of X (i.e., there is no directed path in G from X to any member of **Y**). Then X is independent (in probability) of **Y** conditional on **P**.

The Causal Markov Assumption says that in the toy-train graph, the motion of the caboose is independent of the motion of the engine conditional on the motion of the tender. It says that in Grandmother's house, the state of the TV is independent of the state of the light conditional on whether or not there is a clapping.

The Causal Markov Assumption implies that the joint probability of any set of values of a causally sufficient set can be "factored" into a product of conditional probabilities of the value of each variable on its parents. For example, according to the toy-train graph, the probability that the engine moves, the tender moves, and the caboose moves is this:

pr(caboose moves | tender moves) · pr(tender moves | engine moves)
    · pr(engine moves)

And in Grandmother's house, the probability that there is a clapping and the TV is on and the light is off is this:

pr(light is off | clapping) · pr(TV is on | clapping) · pr(clapping)

Here "pr($x \mid y$)" denotes the probability of x conditional on y.

The Causal Markov Assumption has several justifications, but one is this: Consider any system whatsoever whose causal relations are described by a directed acyclic graph in such a way that the probability of any value of any represented variable is determined (by any function of) the values of its parents in the graph. *If the exogenous variables are independently distributed, then the graph and the joint probability distribution must satisfy the Causal Markov Assumption.*[1]

3.4 Causal Bayes Nets

A directed graph and the Markov Assumption do not themselves determine a unique probability distribution; they only impose a restriction on any probability distribution appropriately associated with the graph. Specialized families of probability distributions can be associated with a graph by specifying parameters that determine how the probability of any value of a variable depends on the values of its direct causes, its parents in the graph. Then a particular probability distribution can be specified by assigning values to the parameters. Specifying parameters whose values give a probability distribution that satisfies the Markov Assumption for the graph is called "parameterizing" the graph.

There are many ways to "parameterize" a graph, and which way is appropriate depends on the subject matter. Some parameterizations determine familiar statistical models—linear regression, logistic regression, factor analytic, "structural equation," etc.—and others do not. For Grandmother's house, for example, where each variable has but two values, a joint probability distribution can be specified by giving a numerical value to each of

pr(light is x | clapping is z)

pr(TV is y | clapping is z)

pr(clapping is z)

for each choice of $x =$ (on/off), $y =$ (on/off), $z =$ (clap/no clap). The idea is just to use the factorization noted previously that is:

pr(light is x, TV is y, clapping is z)

$\quad$ = pr(light is x | clapping is z) · pr(TV is y | clapping is z)

$\quad\quad$ · pr(clapping is z)

Sometimes variables are thought to have some explicit functional dependence on one another. Here is another way to parameterize the same graph. Assume that the state of the light is determined by the state of clapping and some unobserved parameter that is either on or off, and similarly, that the state of the TV is determined by the state of clapping and another unobserved parameter that is either on or off. So we have the following equations:

$L = f(p, \text{Clap})$

$TV = g(q, \text{Clap})$

Since each variable (or parameter) takes only two values, f and g must be Boolean functions. For example, f and g might be multiplication, or Boolean addition, or one might be multiplication and the other addition, etc. Now specify any probability distribution for which p, q, and Clap are independent for all possible assignments of their values. The result is a probability distribution over L, TV, and Clap that satisfies the Markov Assumption. We will consider parametrizations of this kind in chapter 7.

For another example of a parameterization with an explicit functional dependence, consider a "structural-equation model" of the relations among college academic ranking (Rank), average SAT percentiles of entering students (SAT), and dropout rate (Drop), which might look like this:

$SAT = a + b\, \text{Rank} + e$

$Drop = c + d\, \text{SAT} + f$

Here a, b, c, d are real-valued parameters, and e and f are unobserved "noises" and are assumed to be independent. The model corresponds to a parameterization of a family of probability distributions corresponding to a directed graph:

Rank $\longrightarrow$ SAT $\longrightarrow$ Drop

Or if the noises are explicitly represented, then the following directed graph:

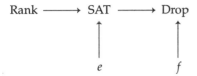

We will consider parameterizations of this kind in chapter 14.

A *Bayes net* is a directed acyclic graph and an associated probability distribution satisfying the Markov Assumption. If the graph is intended to represent causal relations and the probabilities are intended to represent those that result from the represented mechanism, the pair form a *causal Bayes net*.

A great many of the causal models deployed in psychology and the social sciences are some kind of Bayes net. Even feed-forward neural networks are Bayes nets. Many recurrent neural nets are examples of a generalization of Bayes nets that allows cyclic graphs with a generalization of the Markov Assumption (d-separation, discussed in chapters 13 and 14). Unrecognized, Bayes nets and causal Bayes nets are lurking almost everywhere.

3.5   The Utility of Causal Bayes Nets

The value of a representation lies entirely in what can be done with it. With causal Bayes nets we can do the following:

Control   When there are no unobserved common causes, Bayes nets can be used to calculate the value (or probability) of any represented variable, given any combination of interventions that fix the values of other variables but do not otherwise alter the causal structure or conditional probabilities.

Prediction   Bayes nets can be used to efficiently calculate the probability of any value of any represented variable *conditional* on any set of values of any other represented variables.

Discovery   In many cases the causal structure of the world represented in a causal Bayes net, or represented by features of such a net, can be discovered from observations, experiments, and background knowledge.

These three functions are among the capacities any agent—a child, for example—would presumably need to acquire and to exercise for causal competence in everyday life. It seems unlikely that the best computer algorithms, designed for maximal reliability and efficiency with minimal prior information in one-shot learning, are implemented in people, but at the very least, the computer algorithms show what is possible with Bayes net representations. The points bear illustration.

Control

If the causal structure and the probability distribution are known, the probability of any value of any represented variable upon a wide class of interventions that force specified values on other variables can be calculated from a corresponding "factorization" of probabilities. Suppose, for example, that it is known that genotype causes smoking and lung cancer, and that smoking also directly causes lung cancer:

For any values of S, G, and L, the probability distribution can be written thus:

$$\text{pr}(S, G, L) = \text{pr}(L \mid G, S) \cdot \text{pr}(G) \cdot \text{pr}(S \mid G)$$

Suppose that an odd new law is enforced: a random device decides who will and who will not smoke. Given that you smoke, what is the probability of lung cancer that results? We assume an intervention on a variable x removes all edges into x in the causal graph, but does not alter other causal relations or the conditional probabilities of other variables. The trick is that the intervention breaks the influence of genotype on smoking, so that after the intervention the causal structure is this:

The intervention makes G and S independent, but ideally it should leave all other conditional probabilities unchanged. So the probability distribution after the intervention is the following:

$$\text{probafter}(S, G, L) = \text{pr}(L \mid G, S) \cdot \text{pr}(G) \cdot \text{probnew}(S)$$

The last factor on the right changes. If the policy simply prevented smoking, $\text{probafter}(S = \text{yes}, G, L)$ would be zero for all values of G, L, and the probability of any pair of values of G, L would be $\text{probafter}(S = \text{no}, G, L)$.

In cases where not all of the probabilities are known, the theory of interventions on causal Bayes nets shows what interventions are necessary to find them. Suppose some causal structure is thought to have the following form:

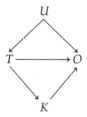

Suppose that the joint probability distribution of T and O is known and U is unobserved. The aim is to discover the influence T has on O, by which I mean the dependence in probability of T on O if T is manipulated and does not influence O through K, but the structure and conditional probabilities are otherwise unchanged. The theory says that probability can be estimated by intervening to fix (or randomize) the value of T while intervening to fix or randomize the value of K. The resulting structure is this:

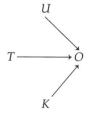

And the probabilities of interest are estimated from the association of O and T then observed.

These simple illustrations correspond pretty exactly to our judgements about control in good scientific method. We randomize treatments because we want to disable any possible common causes of treatment and the outcome under study.[2] We do blind and double-blind studies because we want to block certain lines of influence so that we can correctly estimate others.

Not all of the consequences of the theory of interventions on causal Bayes nets are so banal. Suppose that you know that the following graph describes the causal relations among the variables:

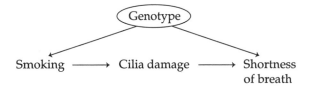

Suppose that associations involving genotype are not observed. The association of smoking and shortness of breath is therefore confounded. Nonetheless, the influence of smoking on shortness of breath can be estimated from the observed associations of the other variables, where, once more, by "influence" I mean the conditional probability distributions of shortness of breath that would result from interventions to fix (or randomize) values of smoking. (A nice presentation of the theory of interventions in Bayes nets is given in Pearl 2000.)

Prediction
The use of Bayes nets for prediction is almost obvious: the Bayes net specifies the joint distribution of the variables as a product of conditional probability distributions. It is not surprising that using the representation, we can compute, by various techniques, the conditional probability of any variable from specifications of the values of any other set of variables. A variety of algorithms have been developed to make such computations efficient.

Table 3.3
Some simple examples of the Markov equivalence classes among three variables and their corresponding independence or conditional-independence relations

$A \perp\!\!\!\perp C \mid B$	$B \perp\!\!\!\perp C \mid A$	$B \perp\!\!\!\perp A \mid C$	$A \perp\!\!\!\perp B$
$A \rightarrow B \rightarrow C$	$B \rightarrow A \rightarrow C$	$B \rightarrow C \rightarrow A$	$A \rightarrow C \leftarrow B$
$A \leftarrow B \rightarrow C$	$B \leftarrow A \rightarrow C$	$B \leftarrow C \rightarrow A$	
$A \leftarrow B \leftarrow C$	$B \leftarrow A \leftarrow C$	$B \leftarrow C \leftarrow A$	

Discovery

We have already seen that distinct causal structures may, either by themselves or with other information, imply distinct-independence and conditional-independence facts. These differences can be exploited in discovery procedures. For example, for 3 variables there are 25 distinct acyclic graphs belonging in 11 distinct equivalence classes; all of the graphs of the same equivalence class imply the same independencies and conditional independencies; any two graphs belonging to distinct classes imply distinct sets of independencies and dependencies. Graphs of the same equivalence class are said to be *Markov equivalent*. The graphs in some equivalence classes are listed in table 3.3, with the set of independencies and conditional independencies characteristic of the class at the top of each column. "$A \perp\!\!\!\perp C \mid B$" means, for all values of A, B, C, A is independent of C conditional on B.

On the assumption that all independencies and conditional indepen-dencies are due to causal structure alone,[3] something can be inferred about the causal structure. How much can be inferred depends on the associations or lack of associations that are found, and on what addi-tional knowledge one has. A great deal can be inferred about causal structure if time order is known and if it is assumed that all common causes are observed. The italicized assumption is sometimes called *faithfulness*, and is essentially a simplicity postulate, although there are various justifications for it. For example, for several parameterizations of a graph, it is almost certain that probability distributions will be faithful to the graph. (See Spirtes et al. 1993, 2001 for discussion and references.)

On the faithfulness assumption, if the only independence relation is $B \perp\!\!\!\perp C \mid A$ and there are no unobserved common causes of observed variables, then the causal relations are one of the three in the second column. If, in addition, one knows (as with clapping at Grandmother's house) that neither B nor C cause A, then the structure $B \leftarrow A \rightarrow C$ is uniquely determined.

The example assumes that $\{A, B, C\}$ is causally sufficient—there is no unobserved confounding cause that influences two or more observed variables—but inferences can also be made from independence and conditional independence when a set of variables is not causally sufficient. Indeed, sometimes it can be discovered from associations that a set of variables is not causally sufficient, because the set of independencies and conditional independencies that hold among those variables alone is incompatible with the Markov Assumption. But we are getting too deeply into details. Suffice it to say that there are efficient algorithms that will extract all of the information about causal structure that can be obtained from independencies, conditional independencies, and background knowledge about what does or doesn't cause what, and that the chief difference in the performance of these algorithms on causally sufficient and causally insufficient sets of variables (in the large-sample limit) is that less causal information can be extracted from insufficient variable sets.[4]

A variety of computational algorithms learn causal relations from background knowledge and data. These procedures—several of which are not "Bayesian" although they learn Bayes nets—were developed specifically for data mining applications, that is, for cases where the complexity of data and the underlying structure are too great for un-aided humans to process reliably. For that very reason the algorithms are unlikely psychological models, but there are a number of much simpler heuristic procedures for learning and modifying networks of causal relations that may have more psychological relevance.

3.6 Heuristics and Concept Formation

Indeterminacy and animacy

The simplest way to learn whether one feature of the world, say X, influences another, say Y, is to manipulate X and see whether and how Y changes. The covariation of X and Y indicates a reliable causal connection only if other causes of Y do not coincide with interventions that vary X, and in particular, only if the association of X and Y is not due to some third common cause of both, Z. We remove (or at least reduce) the chance of coincidental causes by varying X on many occasions. In science we remove (or at least reduce) the chance of a common cause by randomizing the treatment of X; in everyday life we eliminate the chance of a common cause of our intervention and of the variation in Y by a tacit postulate, freedom of the will. Of course, the postulate that our own actions are uncaused by factors that, by separate mechanisms, also bring about circumstances we later observe is not always true, but if we did not tacitly assume as much as an everyday rule of thumb about ourselves, and if it were not generally true to good approximation, we could not get started finding our way around the world, and if we did not tacitly assume as much about others, we could not learn by imitation.

There is more to be learned from manipulating X and observing co-variation of Y than just whether X causes Y. Suppose that we have done that and postulate the following:

Two different cases apply: the presence and absence of Y may be

$$X \longrightarrow Y$$

uniquely determined by interventions that do or do not produce X, or it may not be. The interesting case is when Y is not uniquely determined by X, and that divides into three interesting subcases.

I will code the occurrence of X with 1, and its absence with 0, and similarly for Y. In one case, whenever X is produced, the frequency with which Y occurs increases, but Y does not always occur: $1 > \mathrm{pr}(Y = 1 \mid X = 1) > \mathrm{pr}(Y = 1)$. And, further, whenever X is not produced, Y does not occur: $\mathrm{pr}(Y = 1 \mid X = 0) = 0$. This feature, which we can call imperfect causation without spontaneity, is not a node or link in a Bayes net, but rather a feature of the Bayes net and a concept about aspects of the world the Bayes net describes. But it does suggest a modification of the causal picture, the Bayes net itself, specifically that there is some further unnoticed feature, Z, that either acts to inhibit or prevent X from producing Y, or whose absence makes X insufficient for Y:

Another case is the reverse: intervention to produce X determines the value of Y uniquely, $\mathrm{pr}(Y = 1 \mid X = 1) = 1$, but Y can also occur spon-

$$X \longrightarrow Y \longleftarrow Z$$

taneously, $0 < \text{pr}(Y = 1 \mid X = 0)$. We have perfect causation with spontaneity, and again we have a concept about the causal relations in the Bayes net and a circumstance that suggests the postulation of a further cause, like Z above, this time a cause that produces Y in the absence of X.

Third, we may have imperfect causation with spontaneity: $0 < \text{pr}(Y = 1 \mid X = 0)$ and $1 > \text{pr}(Y = 1 \mid X = 1) > \text{pr}(Y = 1)$. Imperfect causation with spontaneity is again a concept about causal relations rather than a causal relation, but here too it suggests positing additional unnoticed causes, including the possibility that the unnoticed causes may be of two different kinds, one sufficient to produce Y in the absence of X and the other without which (or with which) X is insufficient to produce Y.

We might guess that these distinctions are important to children and even to infants, because imperfect causation with spontaneity is a rough guide to animacy. Inanimate objects tend, on the whole, to be things that children cannot alter, or that they can alter reliably, or if they cannot be altered reliably, that do not alter themselves. Animate objects tend to be unreliably altered and to alter themselves.

Indeterminacy is not the only concept it makes sense to abstract from a network. One can form the concept of the causes of a feature or collection of features, or the concept of the effects of a feature or collection of features. As we will see, these possibilities also lead in some contexts to altering the network.

Learning remote effects

Suppose that manipulating X is imperfectly associated with the occurrence of Y and Z. There are several possible causal arrangements, including (1) to (4):

1. X can cause Y and Z:

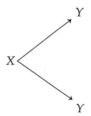

2. X can cause Y, which causes Z, or X can cause Z, which causes Y.

(2.1) $X \longrightarrow Y \longrightarrow Z$

(2.2) $X \longrightarrow Z \longrightarrow Y$

3. X can cause Y and some unobserved factor, say U, can cause Y and Z, or X can cause Z and some unobserved factor can cause Y and Z:

(3.1) $X \longrightarrow Y \longleftarrow U \longrightarrow Z$

(3.2) $X \longrightarrow Z \longleftarrow U \longrightarrow Y$

4. And finally, the two cases (3.1) and (3.2) can be combined with an influence of Y on Z or of Z on Y, respectively.

If X, Y, Z are all indeterministically related, all of these alternative explanations are distinguished from one another by independence or conditional-independence relations. Case 1 and only case 1 implies that Y and Z are independent conditional on X. Case (2.1) and only that case implies that X is independent of Z conditional on Y, and case (2.2) and only that case implies that X is independent of Y conditional on Z. Case (3.1) and only that case implies that X is independent of Z; case (3.2) and only that case implies that X is independent of Y; case (4.1) and case (4.2) imply none of the other independencies or conditional independencies and imply that X is not independent of Y conditional on Z. Cases (4.1) and (4.2) are discussed further in chapter 7 in relation to Cheng models.

If, on the other hand, the values of Y, Z are uniquely determined by the value of X, none of these structures can be distinguished by independence and conditional independence. Of course, time order and spatial relations may provide information that decides the question.

This at least suggests that the existence and structure of indirect effects can be more easily learned if different actions are not too narrowly distinguished by kind but are regarded as a single kind of action (pushing, which can have many strengths, against objects of many weights and frictions, and similarly pulling and kicking, etc.).

Separating causes from covariates

Just as it can be useful for learning not to distinguish kinds of actions too finely, it can be essential to distinguish between kinds of concomitant actions one of which has a kind of effect and the other of which does not. If neither X nor Y causes the other but are both associated with an effect Z, it may be that X alone causes Z, or Y alone causes Z, or both do. If X and Y are not perfectly correlated, we can learn which explanation is correct from conditional independencies. If X alone causes Z, then Y and Z should be independent conditional on X, and symmetrically if Y alone causes Z.

Restructuring causal networks

Since the complexity of learning a network and the complexity of finding the best explanation of a phenomenon and the complexity of prediction all depend on the number of values of variables and on the degree of connectedness of the graph, reducing edges produces computational economy, and eliminating low probability connections saves effort in many contexts.

Suppose that we have a network in which X, Y, Z are direct causes of W. We can simplify the network by collapsing X, Y, Z into a single feature that is some function of the three variables, and thus reduce the number of edges. We cannot do so in general without loss, however. For example, if X, say, is also a cause of another feature R, which is not influenced by Y or Z. In that case, unless Y and Z are perfectly correlated with X, the new variable (for example, X or Y or Z, or $X \& Y \& Z$) will then be a less reliable predictor of R than is X alone.

Collapsing variables with a common effect

Rather than thinking that spherical things roll when pushed, middle-sized things roll when pushed, and solid things roll when pushed,

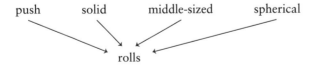

all of which may often be true, one may think that balls roll when pushed:

push   ball

roll

(Here a ball is approximately a spherical middle-sized solid.) We can make a less firm probabilistic inference to "rolling if pushed" from the fact alone that an object is middle-sized or the fact alone that the object is solid, than we can make from the fact that the object is a ball, a feature that may be identified from various conjunctions of observed properties.

Collapsing causes of distinct effects
Separate causes of distinct features can be identified. So, for instance,

$$X \longrightarrow Y \quad Z \longrightarrow W$$

becomes

$$Y \longleftarrow U \longrightarrow W$$

where $U = X = Z$. This sort of thing is especially natural for unobserved but inferred causes. If, for example, an unobserved feature is posited as the cause of spontaneous motion of one kind of object and an unobserved feature is posited as the cause of spontaneous motion of another kind of object, it may be natural and economical to identify the two unobserved features.

Dividing causes and effects
Conversely, a single cause (or effect) can be divided into different features. If first identified as one and the same, the causes of spontaneous motion in people and in machines can later be separated.

Introducing an abstract variable for mutually exclusive features
Suppose that we have a network in which X, Y, Z are mutually exclusive and jointly exhaustive binary variables, that is, in any circumstance one and only one of them has the value 1. Since they are associated, in a graphical representation there must be edges between them (or common causes). We can reduce the number of edges of the network by forming a single variable from the three (or however many) variables. The concept of the color of a surface, and many other concepts, have this feature, although whether the concepts are formed in anything like this way is another matter.

If multiple features are all associated with one another and no conditional independence relations hold among them, any Bayes net, confined to these features alone, is completely connected—there is an edge, in one direction or the other, between every pair of variables. While there are statistical, and no doubt substantive, constraints, it is sometimes possible to simplify such a network by introducing a common cause of all of the variables and removing any edges between them. A single common cause of a set of variables produces associations among all of them but allows no independence or conditional independence relations among the affected variables alone.

Deleting intermediate variables
If a variable is intermediate between others in a network, it can be deleted if appropriate additions are made. For example, the graph on the left becomes the graph on the right:

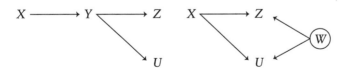

Here U, X, Y, Z are observed and W is unobserved. If W is omitted, however, unless the relation between X and Y is deterministic, there is a loss in such identifications, because Z and U are not independent, conditional on X, according to the graph on the left.

Refining and coarsening variables

A variable that takes only two values (heavy or light, for example) can be refined by introducing further values (heavy, medium, light). A causal feature can be conjoined with another feature, changing a variable with two values into a variable with four values. Conversely, a continuous variable can be coarsened by dividing its values into discrete intervals.

Using prior knowledge

Perhaps the most common and most reliable form of prior knowledge is implicit in inferences from interventions: one knows that the intervention and some immediate effect of the intervention have no common third cause. Almost as common is knowledge of time order, which permits decisions about causal dependence that outweigh strength of association and other factors. If one observes A occurring before B and B before C, the fact that C is more strongly associated with B than is A does not lead one to think that C is the more likely, or stronger, cause of B; instead, one concludes that C is no cause at all of B.

Other, more substantive kinds of prior knowledge are useful in searching for causes. For example, loose analogy: if O is something with an abstract feature A and in other things with abstract feature A a certain causal relation holds, one looks for an analogous causal relation in O, and so on.

Overthrowing prior knowledge

Any system for which it is important to gain causal knowledge as fast as possible is apt to overshoot, to fix on hypothetical causal relations that are entirely wrong, or too general, or too specific, or involve the wrong variables. When evidence builds up that a postulated causal relation is wrong, it may be abandoned, but because causal relations presumed to be known are used in finding others, abandoning any one piece of knowledge may remove the original reasons for adopting other causal relations. The problem of maintaining reasons bites again. But with less venom. The removal of a causal connection in a Bayes net leaves a Bayes net, a system of causal hypotheses that is still self-consistent, can still be used to predict the outcomes of actions, can still be further elaborated and revised. A correct network from which an edge is incorrectly deleted may yield radically wrong predictions, but it at least yields consistent predictions, and the error can be discovered and remedied.

Missing algorithms

There are bits of computer science that provide algorithms for some of these ways of learning and revising causal Bayes nets (Spirtes et al. 1993, 2000; Jordan 1998; Glymour and Cooper 1999). There are certainly no algorithms that synthesize such strategies into a procedure that could be put into a robot that would develop like a baby and not run afoul of the frame problems. But arguably we have some of the pieces for such an algorithm, and arguably the structure of Bayes networks that are calibrated to the actual world helps to solve some aspects of the frame problem more or less automatically. For example, Bayes networks provide efficient ways to determine the relevance of features or variables to new data when the networks are sparse—when most features are unconnected. They may not localize reasons, but they permit localized revision, and they allow rapid prediction in sparse networks. Arguably, the significant causal relations of the actual world are indeed sparse, and it is at least a plausible hypothesis that developing children find that the properties, the "concepts," of their world reveals a sparse structure. Fodor's "fridgeon" problem is transformed into an issue of algorithmic details. (For a very interesting study of causal Bayes nets in adult categorization, quite different from these suggestions, see Rehder 1999.)

3.7 Experiments

The literature on infants and children is that usefully explores general learning procedures like those of the previous section is small, but not completely lacking.

Watson (1979) studied the kicking behavior of infants under a variety of associations of kicking with the motion of a mobile above the baby. He found significantly higher kicking rates when two conditions both obtained: when, after a kick, the probability of the motion of the mobile was high (.75) but less than perfect (<1.0), and when the probability of the motion of the mobile in the absence of a kick was greater than 0 (8 "spontaneous" motions per minute rather than 4 or 0). It is well known in classical and instrumental conditioning that partial reinforcement gives the highest response rate and is the hardest to extinguish. But that regularity applies only to one side of Watson's experiment, and there may reasonably be a further interpretation. Considerable later work suggests connections between children's attributions of mental states to an object, and "spontaneous" changes in the object's state, especially its motion (see Johnson 2000 for a review).

Watson's experiments predate Bayes-net formalism, but they are a virtual application of the ideas of causal Bayes nets. The simplest causal distinction one can make is between features that respond to one's action and features that do not. Watson's infants act on that distinction. Perhaps the second simplest distinction is between kinds of events that follow invariably from one's action and those that do not. Watson's infants act on that distinction. But the really interesting feature of Watson's results is paralleled in a more complicated aspect of causal Bayes nets. We say a causal system described by a Bayes net is *deterministic* if each variable in the network that has an edge directed into it is a deterministic function of its direct causes, as represented in the network. So if the mobile moves if and only if the baby kicks, Bayes net (1) is deterministic: pr(mobile moves | kick) = 1, pr(mobile moves | no kick) = 0.

(1) kick $\longrightarrow$ mobile motion

If the mobile moves when and only when *either* the baby kicks *or* a computer sends a signal, then Bayes net (2) is also a deterministic Bayes net: pr(mobile moves | kick and signal) = pr(mobile moves | kick and no signal) = pr(mobile moves | no kick and signal) = 1; pr(mobile moves | no kick and no signal) = 0.

(2) kick $\longrightarrow$ mobile motion $\longleftarrow$ computer signal

But if the computer signal, while real, is ignored in the representation of network (2), and only the associations between kicking and the mobile motion are recorded, then the causal Bayes net that results looks like (1) but with an *indeterministic* probability: pr(mobile moves | kick) $\neq$ 1, pr(mobile moves | no kick) $\neq$ 0. I (following Spirtes et al. 1993, 2001) say that a causal Bayes net is *pseudoindeterministic* if it has indeterministic relations that derive from ignoring some of the causes in a larger, deterministic network.

Watson suggests that the infants in the condition in which the mobile moves spontaneously and responds indeterministically to kicks are trying to perfect the efficacy of kicking. I suggest two other interpretations. They may be positing an unobserved cause or causes of the motion of the mobile besides their kicking, and exploring the contingencies—experimenting, in other words. Or they may be confirming the extension in their world of an innate distinction between deterministic and non-deterministic systems—a concept that is not a node or link in a causal Bayes net but rather a feature of some nodes in some causal Bayes nets. Or they may be doing both. Rather than debating a priori which of these several interpretations is correct, I think it more important to conduct further experiments suggested by the causal-Bayes-net representation.

For example, how is kicking behavior altered if, in Watson's experiments, a light near the mobile, or some other stimulus, is used as an additional variable? If the spontaneous motion of the mobile is a deterministic function of the light, is the kicking behavior similar to that obtained in Watson's experiment, where there was no apparent cause of the spontaneous motion of the mobile, or is it different? If the motion of the mobile is entirely determined jointly by the infant's kicking and the state of the light, how much does the baby kick? In both of these ways, indeterministic features of the mobile are made conditionally deterministic, and if infants exhibit different kicking behavior than in the case of imperfect causation with spontaneous motion, that would at least suggest that they are already sensitive to some conditional frequency relations.

I know of no experiment that tests whether infants or very young children separate causes from covariates according to the Markov Assumption, that is, using conditional independence. But there is evidence that three- and four-year-olds do.

Gopnik and Sobel (2000) introduced three- and four-year-old children to a "blicket detector"—a small platform that could emit a loud noise and a bright light. The experimenter separately placed each of two small objects on the detector, one of which set off the machine. The subject was told by ostension (not description) that the object which activated the detector was a "blicket." Two new objects were then introduced, one of them physically similar to one of the previous objects and one of them physically similar to the other previous object. The detector was activated only by the new object physically dissimilar to the object that had previously set off the detector. The subjects were asked which of the new objects is a "blicket" and reliably picked the new object that set off the detector rather than the new object that was physically similar to the object that had been previously named a "blicket." The experiment shows—what should be unsurprising—that children can associate sortal terms with causal powers, overcoming any tendency to sort things by the phenomenological properties of the things themselves.

In a related experiment, Gopnik et al. (in press) found that three- and four-year-olds can and do make causal judgements in accord with instances of the Markov condition, specifically that they can sort causally relevant variables from causally irrelevant variables in accordance with conditional-independence relations. Subjects were told that blickets set off the detector and shown examples of an object setting off the detector. An object was subsequently put on the detector with no activation, then removed, a second object was put on the detector with activation, then removed, and both objects put on the detector simultaneously, with activation. The last step was repeated twice more. In a control experiment, the first object was always put on the detector alone and activation resulted in 3 of 4 trials, and the second object was put on the detector alone, with activation in all 4 trials. (See tables 3.4 and 3.5.) Arguably children were merely judging something to be a blicket if it set off the detector sufficiently often when placed on the detector alone, with no other object on the detector. (An easy further control would repeat the experiment with the same frequencies in both conditions but with a third object, Z, always on the detector.)

3.8 Conclusion

Bayes nets are (or can be) a representation of causal relations and probability relations, but they are not themselves algorithms for anything. Yet they form a representation whose structure (the topology of the graph and the connection of that topology with conditional independence through the Markov Assumption) makes several aspects of the frame problem easier to manage. A network can be used to determine

Table 3.4
Experimental condition: children (typically) judge that Y is a blicket but that X is not

X	Y	Blicket Detector
On	Off	Off
Off	On	On
On	On	On
On	On	On
On	On	On

pr(Blicket Detector = on | X = on) = .75
pr(Blicket Detector = on | Y = on) = 1.0
pr(Blicket Detector = on | X = on, Y = on) = 1.0
pr(Blicket Detector = on | X = off, Y = on) = 1.0
pr(Blicket Detector = on | X = on, Y = off) = 0
pr(Blicket Detector = on | X = off, Y = off) = 0
(by background instruction)

Blicket Detector is independent of X conditional on Y.

Table 3.5
Control condition: children (typically) judge that X and Y are both blickets

X	Y	Blicket Detector
On	Off	Off
On	Off	On
On	Off	On
On	Off	On
Off	On	On
Off	On	On
Off	On	On
Off	On	On

pr(Blicket Detector = on | X = on) = .75
pr(Blicket Detector = on | Y = on) = 1.0
pr(Blicket Detector = on | X = on, Y = on) = unknown
pr(Blicket Detector = on | X = off, Y = on) = 1.0
pr(Blicket Detector = on | X = on, Y = off) = .75
pr(Blicket Detector = on | X = off, Y = off) = 0
(by background instruction)

Blicket Detector is not independent of Y conditional on X = off.
Blicket Detector is not independent of X conditional on Y = off.

the conditional probability of one feature or variable from the values of other features or variables, and it can be used to determine the probability of one feature or variable after manipulations that force values on other variables. In both cases, the network structure can be exploited by algorithms sometimes to enormously simplify such determinations. These advantages obtain if the network is sparse and the conditional probabilities can be simply parameterized (for example, if the features don't have very many distinct values or if continuous variables are normally distributed). If we imagine a baby building its causal knowledge in a fashion we can represent as an expanding network or perhaps as a collection of loosely linked networks, however organized, we may suppose that the networks are sparse indeed, and where they are not, mental changes take place that we can usefully describe as reconfiguring a network.

Learning a causal network requires two things: variables and data. An initial set of variables can be transformed in myriad ways, sometimes with resulting simplifications or complexifications in the topology and parameterization of networks that agree with the associations in the data. Variables can be coarsened, refined, combined, omitted, identified with one another, and introduced. The learnability and the simplicity of the causal relations extracted from the data will vary with alterations of the variables, and it seems a reasonable guess that we come into the world wired for properties that have simple and distinctive causal relations of value to us, and that, as we develop, we reconfigure our concepts where necessary to optimize, or at least to satisfice, some combination of simplicity of causal topology and empirical adequacy.

The literature on artificial intelligence as applied to Bayes networks is replete with proposals for coarsening variables, introducing new variables, computing conditional probabilities within a network, computing the effects of interventions in a network, and, of course, procedures for learning networks from observations, experiments, and background knowledge. Many of the procedures have important ideal theoretical properties—they are guaranteed to converge to the right answer under certain assumptions (e.g., the Markov and faithfulness assumptions). The procedures tend to be risk-averse, to demand a lot of data, and to be computationally demanding (in the worst case, all of the correct procedures are nonpolynomial-hard). Rather than showing how children uncover the causal structure of the world, these procedures instead provide rules of thumb and an existence proof: it can be done. But the child's context is different from the data miner's: the child wants answers now, but the child's data will come in vast chunks only as mobility and motor skills develop. The child can risk error now with the prospect of revision later. Developmental psychology should take artificial intelligence back where it started, to android epistemology, to the ambition of building a computational baby.

II

Adult Judgements of Causation

4

A Puzzling Experiment

4.1 The Baker Experiment

A. G. Baker et al. (1993) carried out the following experiment. Adult subjects sat at a computer with a joystick to manipulate. An image of a tank—the shooting kind—appeared on one side of the screen, and a "safe" region on the other side. The subjects were told that between the tank and safety were mines sensitive to color, and that manipulating the joystick as soon as the tank began to move would camouflage the tank. Subjects were asked to indicate on a scale from −100 to +100 their initial estimate of the "efficacy" of the camouflage in getting the tank through the minefield. Subjects were also told that sometimes a plane would appear on the screen, and they were asked to estimate, on the same scale, the efficacy of the plane in getting the tank through the minefield. They were also told that the aim of the exercise was to improve their estimates with experience.

After these preliminaries, the tank would begin to move slowly across the screen, and, if the subject pressed the joystick within a short interval of time, a ray would strike the tank and change its coloring—that is, would camouflage the tank. Camouflaged or not, the tank would move on, and a plane would appear or not. The tank either would be blown up along its passage or would cross the minefield safely. After either conclusion, the screen would be reset, and a new trial would begin. After twenty such trials, the subjects were again asked to estimate the efficacy of the camouflage and the plane. Twenty more trials then followed, after which the subjects gave final estimates of efficacy.

The experiment was conducted with a variety of different actual dependencies for reaching safety on the camouflaging of the tank and the appearance of the plane. In the first arrangement, the experimenters assigned the actual probabilities as follows:

Probability that the tank reaches safety if it is camouflaged = .75
Probability that the tank reaches safety if it is not camouflaged = .25
Probability that the tank reaches safety if the plane appears = 1
Probability that the tank reaches safety if the plane does not appear = 0

For brevity, in the future I will respectively represent these four sentences thus:

$pr(S \mid C) = .75$

$pr(S \mid {\sim}C) = .25$

$pr(S \mid P) = 1$

$pr(S \mid {\sim}P) = 0$

The subjects were not told these probabilities, of course, but they governed the joint frequencies of events in the forty trials.

The subjects camouflaged the tank on about half of the trials. At the end of the experiment, the subjects' averaged judgements of "efficacy" and the standard deviations of their estimates on the -100 to $+100$ scale were as follows:

Efficacy of appearance of the plane = 92 (standard deviation [s.d.] = 5)
Efficacy of camouflage = -6 (s.d. = 8)

On average, the subjects thought the plane was almost perfectly efficacious, and on average they thought the camouflage had no, or almost no, influence at all. These judgements were a considerable change from the subjects' initial opinions, which for the plane averaged -4 (s.d. = 8) and for the camouflage averaged 29 (s.d. = 7).

The interest of the experimenters was in the second result, that at the end of the forty trials the subjects thought the camouflage had no efficacy—indeed, finding that result was the very point of the experiment. The conclusion of the authors is that the subjects' judgements that camouflage had little or no effect were irrational. They claim, without showing, that the subjects' judgements were in accord with a famous model of classical conditioning, the Rescorla-Wagner model, widely used in studies of animal conditioning, where "overshadowing" of smaller causes by bigger causes has often been demonstrated.

Why irrational? In 1980 Lorraine Allan published a discussion of measures of association for binary variables, that is, variables taking only two possible values, as in present or absent, 1 or 0. She argued that the following measure (which has a long prior history) of the association of a cue or indicator or causal variable A with a subsequent variable E is superior to several alternatives:

$$\Delta P_{EA} =_{\text{df}} \text{pr}(E \mid A) - \text{pr}(E \mid \sim A)$$

(Here, and elsewhere, I sometimes abbreviate "$E = 1$" as "E", and "$A = 0$" as $\sim A$, etc.)

In keeping with many other psychologists, Baker et al. take the measure as authoritative not only for associations but also as a measure of the efficacy of A for producing E. Accordingly, in their view, the subjects *ought* to have judged that the efficacy of camouflage was not 0, but $.75 - .25 = .5$. The presence of a more efficacious cause, the plane, overshadowed the efficacy of the camouflage in the subjects' judgement, and the subjects erroneously discounted the effect of the camouflage.

Rescorla and Wagner's model of classical conditioning derives from a tradition of mathematical models of Pavlovian learning. Among psychologists it may well be the most influential model of learning in the last thirty years. The model assumes binary potential causes ($C_1, C_2, \ldots, C_n$) and a binary effect (E), where the two allowed values correspond to presence and absence. Furthermore, it assumes that there is an always-present variable (C_0) representing the causal influence of the constant experimental background. Causal knowledge then consists of knowledge of an associative strength, given by V_i, for each potential cause. The associative strength of C_i with E after case $t + 1$ is defined inductively as $V_i^{t+1} = V_i^t + \Delta V_i^t$, where

$$\Delta V_i^t = \begin{cases} 0 & \text{if cause } C_i \text{ does not appear in case } t; \\[2ex] a_i \beta_1 \left(\lambda - \sum_{\substack{\text{Cause } C_j \text{ appears in case } t}} V_j \right) & \text{if both } C_i \text{ and } E \text{ appear in case } t; \\[2ex] a_i \beta_2 \left(0 - \sum_{\substack{\text{Cause } C_j \text{ appears in case } t}} V_j \right) & \text{if } C_i \text{ appears and } E \text{ does not appear in case } t. \end{cases}$$

Here a_i is a unitless parameter representing the salience of C_i to the reasoner relative to the saliencies of the other potential causes, β_1 and β_2 represent learning rates respectively for cases in which the effect does or does not occur, and λ is the maximum level of associative strength possible, and in animal experiments, is usually thought to be proportional to the intensity of the outcome. The Rescorla-Wagner model simply states that, after a particular case, we update the strength of each potential cause, V_i, by ΔV_i^t. If the potential cause i is absent in a case, then ΔV_i^t is 0. If the potential cause does appear, then ΔV_i^t is proportional to the difference between (a) the sum of the current causal strengths of the appearing causes and (b) either 0 or λ, depending on whether the effect occurred.

We can make sense of the notion of an *equilibrium set of values* for the RW process if we assume a probability distribution over the various possible combinations of present and absent cues and a conditional probability for E, given any combination of present and absent cues. For example, in the Baker experiment, we can infer the following probabilities:

$pr(C, P, S) = .375$

$pr(C, P, \sim S) = 0$

$pr(C, \sim P, S) = 0$

$pr(C, \sim P, \sim S) = .125$

$pr(\sim C, P, S) = .125$

$pr(\sim C, P, \sim S) = 0$

$pr(\sim C, \sim P, S) = 0$

$pr(\sim C, \sim P, \sim S) = .375$

An equilibrium is then a set of values V_i for all of the cues for which the *expected value* of each ΔV_i is zero. When there is a single possible cue X besides the constant cue, the RW model has a unique equilibrium value for the association strength of that cue, and it is equal to Allan's ΔP. But when there are more than one possible variable cue, as in the Baker experiment, whether there is a unique equilibrium or several equilibria depends on the probability distribution over the joint occurrences and absences of the cues and E—the cue-and-outcome patterns. Patricia Cheng (1997) characterized, in other terms, the equilibrium association values for special probability distributions. David Danks (2001) has since supplied a general algorithm for finding the equilibria and has provided necessary and sufficient conditions for the existence of a unique equilibrium. His results agree with Cheng's when the conditions for her analysis apply. And when there *is* a unique equilibrium, it is generally not given by setting $V_i = \Delta P_i$. In particular, for the probabilities just given for the Baker experiment, the unique equilibrium is $V_C = 0$ and $V_P = 1$, agreeing quite well with the subjects' mean judgements that the camouflage has no, or almost no, influence on reaching safety, while the appearance of the plane is almost certain to result in a safe arrival.

What's missing? The analysis given by Baker et al. seems complete. They conclude that the RW model and other "associative models" may not be the whole story, but they explain human performance in the learning task in their experiment: "It is certainly possible that these associative mechanisms are part of a hybrid mechanism involving both associative mechanisms and more representational, retrospective processes." But no representational process is needed for this experiment.

4.2   Of Mice and Men

The Baker experiment and its interpretation leave a puzzle: if people are not rational in their learned causal judgements, even in this rather easy problem, how do they manage to learn to get around in the rather messier real world; how do they learn to predict and influence what will happen when they, or someone else, takes an action? Even if people were born with complete causal knowledge of the world, it seems that the moral of the Baker experiment and its interpretation is that experience would lead them irrationally to abandon their knowledge in favor of erroneous judgements of efficacy. Something is wrong.

An obvious thought is that Baker et al. are wrong about what rationality requires. Allan's arguments, as they construe them, that ΔP is the quantity that measures the strength of a causal influence, seem less than decisive. In many cases, when there are multiple potential causes, judging the influence of one potential cause by ΔP is obviously wrong, and a fundamental principle of experimental design and statistical analysis is either to control other potential causes by arranging circumstances so that they do not vary or to control other potential causes statistically by looking only at a set of cases in which, for each potential alternative cause, there is a fixed value that the potential cause has for all of the cases in the set. This procedure is often referred to as *conditioning* on the alternative potential causes. Perhaps that is how the efficacy of a potential cause should be judged. Perhaps ΔP is the wrong measure in the context of this experiment.

In that rarest of things, a charming psychological essay, Barbara Spellman (1996b) claims as much. She suggests that when there is more than one potential cause of an outcome, in judging the efficacy of a potential cause one should condition on other, perhaps *all*, potential causes. Suppose, to use her example, one is to judge the influence on growth of the application to plants of a red liquid from experimental trials in which sometimes the red liquid alone is applied, sometimes the red liquid and another, blue liquid, are both applied, and sometimes only the blue liquid is applied. In that case, she says, one should calculate ΔP for the red liquid using only those trials in which the blue liquid was not applied or, alternatively, only those trials in which the blue liquid was applied. In two experiments she describes, subjects behaved as though they were doing exactly that. And in fact, the subjects' judgements of the efficacy of the red liquid agree with RW equilibria for her experiments.

Now consider the Baker experiment. In cases in which the plane is absent, the outcome is the same whether the tank is camouflaged or not—the tank never reaches safety. ΔP for camouflage, conditional on the absence of the plane, hereafter, $\Delta P_{CS;\,\sim P}$, is 0. And in cases in which the plane is present, the outcome is the same whether the tank is camouflaged or not—the tank always reaches safety. $\Delta P_{CS;\,\sim P}$ is 0, and so is $\Delta P_{CS;\,P}$. By Spellman's lights, Baker's subjects were behaving rationally.

Two questions make this response not entirely unsatisfactory. *Why* should one conditionalize; why is the conditional ΔP, rather than the simple unconditional ΔP, the right estimate of the efficacy of the red liquid or the camouflage? Absent an answer to that question, one might regard Spellman's experiments as just another demonstration of human irrationality. And the second question is, *What* should one condition on? Spellman doesn't say. In her experiment the other potential cause, the blue liquid, had two values: poured on and not poured on. Should ΔP for the red liquid be estimated conditioning on the blue liquid being poured, or on the blue liquid not being poured? As in the Baker experiment, the probabilities in her experiment were arranged so that it made no difference, but that is not necessarily, or even usually, the case. If the house-current circuit breaker is on, the lamp goes on if and only if the light switch is turned on, but if the house circuit breaker is off, the lamp is off no matter the position of the light switch. ΔP for the lamp switch, conditional on the circuit breaker being on, is 1; ΔP for the lamp switch, conditional on the circuit breaker being off, is 0. And, more generally, should one condition on *all* of the other potential causes, or just some of them, and if only some of them, which ones and why? Evidently, that depends on whether, when reporting the "efficacy" of a potential cause, subjects are reporting only its direct effect on the outcome through mechanisms that do not include other potential causes under consideration, or are instead reporting its total effect on the outcome, including any effects through mechanisms that do include other potential causes under consideration. Here is another example. Turning the lamp switch on causes the light to go on, which causes the radiometer to turn. If we consider only the state of the lamp switch and the state of the light, what are their respective "efficacies" for turning the radiometer? For the lamp switch, it depends on what is meant: directly, without the light, it has no efficacy at all; indirectly, through causing the light to go on, it has an effect. If the total effect of the lamp switch is wanted, we had better not condition on the state of the light. But there are deeper difficulties with Spellman's proposal.

We can see these further difficulties with Spellman's analysis by imagining more complicated variations of the Baker experiment. We arrange things so the joystick influences whether the tank is camouflaged and also influences whether the plane appears. Suppose that when the joystick is moved to on, camouflaging always occurs but never occurs otherwise. When the joystick is moved to on and a random variable R unobserved by the subjects (and whose existence is unknown to them) is on, the plane appears 90 percent of the time; otherwise it does not appear. When the random variable R has the value on, the tank reaches safety 90 percent of the time; otherwise it does not reach safety. The plane's appearance or absence actually has no influence on whether the tank reaches safety. Camouflaging has no influence at all on whether the tank reaches safety. Suppose that the randomizer is on 90 percent of

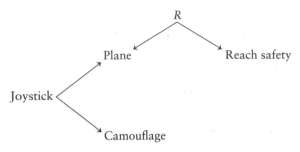

Figure 4.1
Actual causal connections in an imaginary experiment

the time, and the subjects move the joystick to the on position 50 percent of the time. We can diagram the actual arrangements as in figure 4.1.

The relevant quantities can be computed from the probabilities alone, but the diagram, which together with the probabilities is a Bayes net, provides an algorithm for the computation (see Pearl 1988). The probability that the tank reaches safety given that the plane appears is .9. The probability that the tank reaches safety given that the plane does not appear is .75. ΔP for the plane is .15. The probability that the tank reaches safety given that the tank is camouflaged is .81. The probability that the tank reaches safety given that the tank is not camouflaged is also .81. The unconditional ΔP for the camouflage is 0, which in this case is the right measure of the influence of the camouflage on whether the tank reaches safety. And what about the quantities Spellman recommends, the ΔP values for camouflage conditional on the plane being present or conditional on the plane being absent, e.g., $\mathrm{pr}(S \mid C, P) - \mathrm{pr}(S \mid {\sim}C, P)$? The first of these quantities, ΔP for camouflage conditional on the plane being present, is not defined in this case. (Because the plane appears only if the tank is camouflaged, the probability that the tank reaches safety given that the tank is not camouflaged and the plane appears is undefined—probabilities conditional on an event of 0 probability are undefined.) The probability that the tank reaches safety given that the tank is camouflaged and the plane does not appear is .42. The probability that the tank reaches safety given that the tank is not camouflaged and the plane does not appear is .81. So ΔP for camouflage given that the plane does not appear is $-.39$!

If subjects follow Spellman's norm, they would say either that the efficacy of camouflage cannot be determined, or that it is $-.39$, or perhaps they would just be uncertain. If they follow Allan's norm, which Baker et al. endorse, they would give the right answer, that the camouflage does not influence whether the tank reaches safety.

What if the conditional ΔP values are both defined but not necessarily equal? Here is another example. Add a second unobserved randomizer Q that influences only whether the tank is camouflaged. Let the probability that the tank is camouflaged be .9 if either Q is on or the joystick is in the on position, or both, and 0 otherwise, and let the probability that Q is on be .5. Leave everything else the same as in the thought experiment just described. ΔP_{PS} for the plane is unchanged from the previous imaginary experiment. ΔP_{CS} for camouflage is also unchanged, 0. The probability that the tank reaches safety given that the plane appears and the tank is camouflaged is .9. The probability that the tank reaches safety given that the plane appears and the tank is not camouflaged is the same, .9. So $\Delta P_{CS;P}$ for camouflage, conditional on the appearance of the plane, but not conditional on the absence of the plane is 0. The probability that the tank reaches safety given that the plane does not appear and the tank is camouflaged is .70. The probability that the tank reaches safety given that the plane does not appear and the tank is not camouflaged is .80. $\Delta P_{CS;\sim P}$ for camouflage, conditional on the absence of the plane, is not 0 but rather $-.10$. The other answer, 0, obtained either by not conditioning at all or by conditioning on the presence of the plane, is correct.

Allan's general rule, on which Baker et al. rely in their experiment, cannot generally be the right normative measure of the efficacy of a potential cause. In cases in which there are two or more potential causes, X and Y, say, one of which, say Y, is an actual cause of the outcome variable and the other of which, X, has no influence on the outcome variable but is itself an effect of Y, Allan's measure of efficacy, ΔP, will wrongly attribute an efficacy to X. (And this is not the only kind of case in which Allan's measure is plainly wrong.) The RW model predicts the average of the subjects' performance in the Baker experiment, which does not obey the Allan norm, ΔP. Spellman's normative measure of efficacy, ΔP conditional on other potential causes, gives no measure of the efficacy of camouflage conditional on the presence of the plane in the first imaginary variation of the Baker experiment and gives the wrong answer conditional on the absence of the plane. And Spellman's normative measure gives two different results in the second imaginary version of the Baker experiment, one plainly right (0) and the other plainly wrong (−.10). (Spellman suggests taking an average in the case of conflicting conditional ΔP values, which would not help in this case.) And finally, Allan's measure, the simple unconditional ΔP, gives the plainly right measure of the efficacy of camouflage in the two imaginary experiments. What a mess! We are left without any basis for judging whether or not the subjects in the Baker experiment correctly learned the efficacy of camouflage. But it at least seems clear that the psychologists are in a perplex.

The problems are not confined to the particular authors I have cited: Allan, Baker, Rescorla and Wagner, and Spellman. Papers testing human judgements of efficacy and comparing them with such "normative" measures as ΔP, conditional ΔP, or related quantities abound in the psychological literature. For example, Cheng and Novick (1990) propose ΔP conditional on the absence of potential causes in an unspecified "focal set" of alternative potential causes, and Melz et al. (1993) elaborate on the proposal this way:

> In assessing conditional contingencies, heuristics are required to determine which tests (of those possible, given the cue combinations that are actually presented) should in fact be performed. We assume, on the basis of the arguments presented earlier, that people prefer to conditionalize the contingency for each target factor on the simultaneous absence of all conditionalizing cues. If this is not possible, then they will conditionalize on the absence of as many conditionalizing cues as possible. (1993, 1404)

And lest there be any doubt that they are talking about selecting the "focal set" referred to in Cheng and Novick (1990), they say,

> Following Cheng and Novick's (1990) terminology, we call the set of events over which a subject computes a particular contingency a focal set.... These may include the universal focal set of all events in the experiment (i.e., the unconditional contingencies) and more restricted focal sets (i.e., conditional contingencies). (1993, 1404)

This suggestion for finding the correct focal set would produce the wrong answer in both of our thought experiments.

Most discussions of psychological measurement of causal efficacy, whether in the Baker experiment or elsewhere, are unclear about what measures of "efficacy" are to measure. Pearl (2000, chap. 9) provides several clear senses of causal strength in terms of Bayes nets and interventions, and Cheng (1997), whose theory will be discussed in chapter 7 of this book, provides another. We will see there that further ambiguities remain. What should be clear, however, is that a *general* rule for estimating causal strength by ΔP cannot correspond to anything normative, and any normative rule for estimating causal strength by some function of a conditional ΔP will require some intricacy in how to specify the "focal" set.

5

The Puzzle Resolved

We recall the Baker experiment: subjects can manipulate a joystick, which camouflages a tank moving across a video screen. Sometimes a plane appears and sometimes not. Sometimes the tank crosses safely and sometimes not. Subjects also know a time order of events: setting the joystick position precedes camouflaging the tank, which precedes the appearance of the plane.

Given the cover story, given the fact that the subjects see a mechanism by which joystick manipulation camouflages the tank, and given the order of appearance of events, there are 16 possible causal pictures the subjects might reasonably have entertained before the experimental trials. Here are some of them:

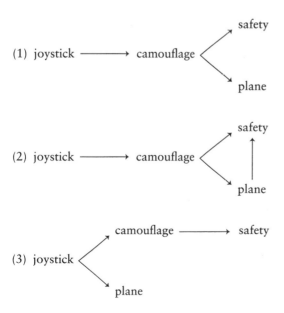

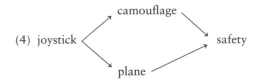

(4) joystick
camouflage
plane
safety

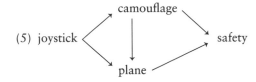

(5) joystick
camouflage
plane
safety

(6) joystick ⟶ camouflage ⟶ plane ⟶ safety

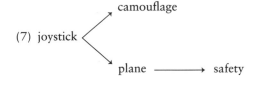

(7) joystick
camouflage
plane ⟶ safety

(8) joystick
camouflage

plane ⟶ safety

(9) joystick
camouflage ⟶ safety

plane

(10) joystick
camouflage ⟶ safety

plane

With C standing for camouflage, P for plane, S for reaching safety, and $\sim$ for the absence of these conditions, the probabilities in the experimental set up are these:

$pr(C, P, S) = .375$

$pr(C, P, \sim S) = 0$

$pr(C, \sim P, S) = 0$

$pr(C, \sim P, \sim S) = .125$

$pr(\sim C, P, S) = .125$

$pr(\sim C, P, \sim S) = 0$

$pr(\sim C, \sim P, S) = 0$

$pr(\sim C, \sim P, \sim S) = .375$

Subjects learn in addition that the tank is camouflaged if and only if the joystick is put in the on position in the appropriate time interval, and the position of the joystick is correlated with the appearance of the plane. Hence they know or can learn several facts from the experimental trials, including these:

• Camouflage and joystick position are independent of reaching safety conditional on the appearance of the plane.
• Camouflage is independent of the plane conditional on the joystick position (in the appropriate time interval—hereafter assumed without remark).
• The plane's appearance is not independent of camouflage.
• The plane's appearance is not independent or conditionally independent of safety.

Structures 6 and 7, and only these structures, explain these facts and the observed associations. Structure 1, for example, implies that the plane is independent of safety, conditional on camouflage. Structure 2 implies that camouflage is not independent of safety, conditional on the plane, and so on.

Structure 6 is consistent with the fact that camouflage is independent of the plane, conditional on the joystick position only because in the experiment the two variables, camouflage and joystick position, are deterministically related, so that the value of either variable uniquely determines the value of the other variable. For structure 6, ΔP measures the difference in the probability of reaching safety on an *intervention* that brings about camouflage and on an intervention that prevents camouflage. (In Pearl's [2000] classification, ΔP is in this case the probability that camouflage is a necessary and sufficient cause of safety.) If, however, subjects' judgements of the "efficacy" of camouflage report something about their estimates of the strength of the *direct* influence of camouflage on safety, through mechanisms that are not blocked by holding constant other variables, then in structure 6 ΔP is surely the wrong measure, for if the presence (or absence) of the plane were held constant, according to structure 6 interventions that change the presence or absence of camouflage would make no difference to reaching safety. In the latter case, Spellman's measure would be more appropriate, and subjects would be entirely rational to judge that the plane has an influence on safety but that camouflage does not.

In structure 7, which fits the associations and independence and conditional independence relations in the probability distribution used in the experiment, camouflage has no influence on safety, but the plane has a direct influence. ΔP_{CS} is not zero, even though camouflage has no influence on reaching safety. Conditional ΔP for camouflage given the plane, $\Delta P_{CS;P}$ (or $\Delta P_{CS;\sim P}$), in this case measures the difference in the probability of reaching safety given an intervention that camouflages the tank and given an intervention that does not camouflage the tank, when the appearance (or absence) of the plane is held constant. That difference is zero. In contrast, there is no difference between the unconditional ΔP of the plane and safety and their ΔP conditional on the state of camouflage, that is $\Delta P_{PS;C} = \Delta P_{PS;\sim C} = \Delta P_{PS}$, and the quantity is positive.

When we represent the alternative causal explanations as Bayes nets and apply the Causal Markov Assumption, the Baker experiment resolves into a variety of possibilities, and which of them conforms to the subjects' understanding is underspecified by the experimental design. The ambiguities concern what causal structures are reasonably inferred from the background stories and data that subjects are given, and to what feature of causal relations subjects respond when they report a judgement of "efficacy."

Consider again the first imaginary experiment from chapter 4. When and only when the joystick is moved to on, camouflaging occurs. When the joystick is moved to on *and* a random variable R unobserved by the subjects (and whose existence is unknown to them) is on, the plane appears 90 percent of the time; otherwise it does not appear. When the random variable R has the value on, the tank reaches safety 90 percent of the time; otherwise it does not reach safety. The appearance or absence of the plane actually has no influence on whether the tank reaches safety. Camouflaging has no influence at all on whether the tank reaches safety. Suppose that the randomizer is on 90 percent of the time and the subjects move the joystick to the on position 50 percent of the time. Joystick is independent of safety; joystick is not independent of safety conditional on the plane; camouflage is independent of safety; camouflage is dependent on safety conditional on the plane; camouflage is independent of safety conditional on the plane and the joystick. Time order is as in the Baker experiment.

Consider versions of Spellman's normative recommendations, according to what one conditions on:

$\Delta P_{CS} = 0$

$\Delta P_{JS} = 0$

$\Delta P_{CS;J} = $ undefined

$\Delta P_{CS;\sim J} = $ undefined

$\Delta P_{CS;P} = 0$

$\Delta P_{CS;\sim P} = 0$

$\Delta P_{CS;PJ} = $ undefined

$\Delta P_{CS;\sim P \sim J} = $ undefined

$\Delta P_{CS;\sim PJ} = $ undefined

$\Delta P_{CS;P \sim J} = $ undefined

Which of these is the correct estimate of the "efficacy" of camouflage? Should subjects say that camouflage has no influence, or a negative influence, or that they cannot tell? There is an explanation that implies all the independencies specified, and that is consistent with the associations and the time order of events and the Causal Markov Assumption:

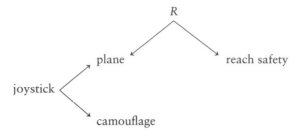

Here *R* is unobserved. Camouflage has no influence on whether the tank reaches safety. The second imaginary experiment has essentially the same features, except that all of the Δ*P* quantities are defined and there is a unique Rescorla-Wagner equilibrium, which is not 0 if the state of the joystick is not among the cues but is 0 if the joystick is included among the cues. Causal Bayes net representations disentangle the various contending normative analyses.

There are three further points. First, in these real and imaginary examples all that is essential for determining the correct answer—that the camouflage has no influence or no direct influence—is knowledge of the time order and which variables are independent conditional on which sets of other variables. Measures of the strength of association other than Δ*P* or conditional Δ*P* would do quite as well for that judgement so long as they conformed to the appropriate independencies and conditional independencies. (In a later chapter we will consider a different measure, Cheng's, and the implications of the Causal Markov Assumption for her theory.) Second, while the Rescorla-Wagner model agrees with one normative answer and with the judgements of experimental subjects in the Baker experiment, normative answers sometimes disagree with the Rescorla-Wagner model. The second imaginary experiment provides an example, but there are much simpler examples. The next chapter discusses how Bayes nets may yield a simple test of the RW model. And third, the imaginary experiments in this chapter illustrate cases in which the application of the Causal Markov Assumption can yield conclusions that there are unobserved causes at work: from the data and initial knowledge provided to subjects in our imaginary experiments, various computer programs could discover that there is an unmeasured cause—*R* in this discussion—of the appearance of the plane and the tank's reaching safety.

6

Marilyn vos Savant Meets Rescorla and Wagner

6.1 Introduction

The Rescorla-Wagner model has dominated psychological theories of human and animal learning for many years, with vast influence. A variety of empirical objections have been made to it, for example, that it neglects learning about a "cue" that happens when the subject observes the effect in the absence of the cue, and that to save the phenomena it requires different parameter settings for similar experimental situations. I will add another, at least hypothetically. There is a very simple case in which the Rescorla-Wagner model predicts that a learner will converge toward associating a "cue" with an outcome when in fact the cue has no influence on the outcome and, further, when the data provided to the learner contain that very information—if the Causal Markov Assumption is made.

6.2 Conditional Dependence and the Monte Hall Game

When two independently distributed variables, say X and Z, both influence a third variable, say Y, then *conditional on some value of* Y, X and Z are not independent. Judea Pearl gives the following illustration. Suppose that the variables are the state of the battery in your car (charged/dead), the state of the fuel tank (not empty/empty), and whether your car starts (starts/does not). Suppose that you regard the states of the battery and of the fuel tank as independent: knowing the state of the battery gives no information about the state of the fuel tank, and vice versa. Now, condition on a value of the effect—whether the car starts— by supposing that you are given the information that your car does not start. *Now* the information that your battery is charged does provide information about the state of the fuel tank.

The general principle is that in a causal graph, if edges from two independent variables (or variables conditionally independent on other variables) are both into, collide with, a third variable, then the two causes are *dependent*, conditional on their effect (and on whatever other variables had to be conditioned on to make the causes independent). The principle is necessary in all linear models, and in all other models satisfying the Causal Markov Assumption and the faithfulness assumption. The latter assumes that all independencies and conditional independencies among a set of variables are implied by the Causal Markov Assumption for the graph describing the causal relations among the variables.

The collider principle is elementary to auto mechanics, but there is anecdotal evidence that people do not recognize it in some contexts, and that many professional statisticians do not recognize it at all. The principle is violated in all regression algorithms, sometimes with strikingly unfortunate results. For example, in a procedure that appears to violate this principle, the estimates of low-level lead exposure on the intelligence of children were obtained by step-wise regression, with the result that the published estimates of the malign effect are probably at least 50 percent too low (Scheines and Boomsma 1999). Other anecdotal evidence comes from Marilyn vos Savant, who for many years ran one of the few intelligent newspaper features, a puzzle and advice column in a Sunday supplement. Vos Savant described, and gave the correct answer to, the Monte Hall problem.

The Monte Hall game goes like this: Before the contestant arrives, the host, Monte Hall, places a thousand dollars behind one door and a (quiet) goat behind each of two other doors. The contestant enters and is told that if she chooses the correct door, she will win the money. The contestant then chooses. Monte Hall then opens one of the doors that the contestant did not choose and that does not contain the money. (If the contestant chose a door that does not contain the money, then Monte Hall has no choice as to which door to open; if the contestant choose the door that does contain the money, then Monte Hall opens one of the other doors at random.) Now, after a door without the money has been opened, the contestant is given the option of changing the choice of doors. What should the contestant do, stick with the first choice, change, or does it not matter? The answer is that the contestant should change doors, and by doing so increases the chance of winning from 1/3 to 2/3. The majority of people presented with the game think it does not matter whether the choice is changed or not, and when vos Savant published her correct answer, she received scores of denunciations, many from professors of statistics.

The Monte Hall problem is an instance of the collider phenomenon—of independent variables conditional on a common effect. Monte Hall's original choice of where to put the money (a variable with three values) and the contestant's original choice of which door has the money (another variable with three values) influence which door Monte Hall opens (still another variable with three values). The contestant's original choice is independent of where Monte Hall put the money. But conditional on the information about which door Monte Hall opened, the contestant's original choice provides information about which door Monte Hall put the money behind.

The anecdotal evidence does not decide the question of whether people can and do make causal judgements in accord with conditional association. In the Monte Hall game, it is not obvious how to identify the variables, and contestants have no data from which to learn, so an explicit analysis was required.

6.3   Testing Rescorla and Wagner's Model

Consider the following structure:

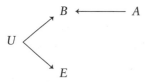

A has no influence at all on *E*, and by the Causal Markov Assumption, *A* and *E* are independent. But *A* and *E* are dependent, conditional on some value of *B*. Now suppose that *U* is not observed. *A*, *B*, and *E* are observed, *A* and *B* precede *E*, and the following associations hold:

- *A* and *B* are dependent.
- *B* and *E* are dependent.
- *A* and *E* are independent.
- *A* and *E* are dependent, conditional on some value of *B*.

If we assume faithfulness and the Causal Markov Assumption, these facts and the time order are inconsistent with any causal pathway from *A* to *E*. If we made inferences in accord with these principles, we would conclude that *A* has no influence on *E*. Indeed, in principle, we could further infer that there is some unobserved factor influencing both *B* and *E*.

If subjects follow the RW model, they will ignore the fact that *A* and *E* have no association and will focus on the fact that *A* and *E* are associated, conditional on a value of *B*. If subjects make judgements in accord with the Causal Markov Assumption and faithfulness, the fact that *A* and *E* are not associated will lead them to judge there is no causal connection between those variables.

Consider the following parameterization:

Experimental setup 1: $A \rightarrow B \leftarrow U \rightarrow E$

$\text{pr}(U = E) = 1$

$\text{pr}(A = 1) = .1$

$\text{pr}(E = 1) = .45$

$\text{pr}(B = 1 \mid A = 1, E = 1) = .8$

$\text{pr}(B = 1 \mid A = 1, E = 0) = .98$

$\text{pr}(B = 1 \mid A = 0, E = 1) = .02$

$\text{pr}(B = 1 \mid A = 0, E = 0) = .35$

One could, as in the Baker experiment, give subjects a substantial number of trials according to this probability distribution and ask for their judgement of "efficacy" or some such thing. A better design, it would seem, would be to also give subjects a second set of trials in which a distinct cue *C* is paired with the same cue *B* as before and the same effect *E*, but *C* actually causes *E*, and at equilibrium $V_C < V_A$. Then subjects may be given a forced choice between *A* and *C* to bring about *E*, with a reward if they succeed in producing *E*. On the assumption that subjects are near equilibrium at the end of each of the two sets of trials, the causal interpretation of the Rescorla-Wagner model requires that subjects prefer to try to bring about E by bringing about A. If they use the Causal Markov Assumption and faithfulness, they should prefer to try to bring about E by bringing about C.

The graph for the second set of trials is simply this:

$$B \longleftarrow C \longrightarrow E$$

For this set of trials, consider the following parameterization:

Experimental setup 2: $B \leftarrow C \rightarrow E$

$\mathrm{pr}(C = 1) = .1$

$\mathrm{pr}(B = 1 \mid C = 1) = .9$

$\mathrm{pr}(B = 1 \mid C = 0) = .2$

$\mathrm{pr}(E = 1 \mid C = 1) = .7$

$\mathrm{pr}(E = 1 \mid C = 0) = .42$

Using Dank's algorithm for computing Rescorla-Wagner equilibria (which can be found at http://srdcc3.ucsd.edu/~ddanks), we obtain the equilibrium values for V_A from the first experiment, which we can compare with the equilibrium values for V_C from the second experiment for various values of the learning parameters β_1 and β_2 (setting $\lambda = 1$ in all cases). These values are given in table 6.1. Whenever β_1 is greater than or equal to β_2, V_A is greater than V_C. Thus, in such circumstances, the

Table 6.1
Equilibrium values for V_A from the first experiment and V_C from the second experiment for various values of the learning parameters β_1 and β_2

β_1	β_2	V_A	V_C
1.0	1.0	0.32	0.29
1.0	0.5	0.433	0.246
0.5	0.5	0.35	0.29
0.1	0.1	0.35	0.29
0.5	1.0	0.245	0.28
1.0	0.1	0.373	0.088
0.1	1.0	0.07	0.12

causal interpretation of the Rescorla-Wagner model predicts that given sufficient evidence, subjects will judge that bringing about A is more likely to cause E than is bringing about C, even though, in fact, A has no influence on E.

Ahmad Hashem and Gregory Cooper (1996) at the University of Pittsburgh tested whether medical residents made causal judgements in accordance with causal Bayes nets, giving them numbers for conditional probabilities rather than data and including a case structurally like those considered here. The medical residents did not do very well with three variables, but because of a data artifact, neither did a Bayes-net learning algorithm. For a comparison with Rescorla-Wagner, it is essential to give subjects data rather than numerical probabilities. A principal difficulty in such an experiment is that a large number of trials is required to approximate the relevant statistics. In two experiments related to those proposed here, David Danks and Craig Mckenzie (Danks 2001) found that among subjects willing to make any causal attributions at all, the modal response is in agreement with the causal Bayes net, although there is a great deal of individual variation, which can in some measure be modeled by varying parameters in the search algorithms to be described in chapter 8. Almost none of the subjects made judgements in accord with the Rescorla-Wagner model.

7

Cheng Models

7.1 Introduction

The most interesting and novel recent psychological account of adult judgements of causation has been developed by Patricia Cheng (1997) and her collaborators (Cheng and Novick 1999). Cheng argues that the account uniquely captures many of the phenomena of adult judgement, but even if it does not, it is a brilliant piece of mathematical metaphysics.

Nancy Cartwright (1989) proposed that there are in the world various fundamental capacities of kinds of events or circumstances. *The capacity of a kind of circumstance C to bring about another kind of circumstance E is the probability of E conditional on C and on the absence of all other potential causes of E.* Ordinary objects in our everyday world are amalgams of components with fundamental capacities. Cheng's psychological theory of our tacit causal theories is a generalization of that idea: we judge instances of kinds to have causal powers to produce or to prevent kinds of effects; the powers can act separately or, in some cases, they may interact. We make minimal assumptions about our world that enable us often to form judgements of causal powers, which in turn we can use in prediction. That is the psychological theory for which Cheng has provided evidence. I am concerned here with using Bayes-net methods to unravel implications of the theory that have not yet been tested. Cheng's models of our models of causation turn out to be Bayes nets under a particular parameterization, which means that we can use what is known about search and estimation for Bayes nets to extend Cheng's theoretical results.

7.2   Cheng's Model of Human Judgement of Generative Causal Power

The metaphysics of Cheng's theory can be viewed as an anatomy of kinds of causal relationships. Cheng considers only causal factors that have two values, present or absent, and only the presence of a factor can have a causal role. She divides causal relations into two sorts: generative and preventive. Generative causal factors increase the probability of an effect, and preventive causal factors decrease it, both subject to appropriate conditions. Causal powers are further divided into the simple and the compound, or interactive. Instances of two or more simple causal powers for the same kind of effect produce an instance of that effect independently of one another. That is, if A and B have simple, non-interactive, generative causal powers to produce E, then when A and B are both present, A may cause E, or B may cause E, or both may separately cause E. The probability that A, if A occurs, *causes* E (which is *not* the probability of E given A) is independent (in probability) of the probability that B, if B occurs, causes E. When A and B generatively interact, the effect may be produced by A alone, by B alone, by both acting separately, or by A and B acting conjointly. Similar relationships apply when one or both causes are preventive or when their interaction tends to prevent E.

That is the metaphysics, and it may seem to many philosophers and statisticians an unpromising basis for a normative, let alone descriptive, theory of causal judgement that is both a real guide in life and has real empirical content. As we will see, there is a good case to be made for it.

Given data on the joint frequency of candidate causes (of effect E) and of E, when unobserved causes of E may also be acting, how do people judge the efficacy or causal power of any particular observed candidate cause? Suppose that they know, or believe, that all unobserved causes of E are generative, and that one or more generative candidate causes of E are observed along with E. Consider the simplest case in which there is one observed generative causal factor, C, and one unobserved generative causal factor, U. In that case, E occurs if and only if *either C occurs and C causes E or if U occurs and U causes E.*

We let the parameter q_{ce} represent the proposition that *C causes E, given that C occurs.* And analogously for q_{ue}. The q parameters have two possible values; 1 represents that the causal factor, if it occurs, acts to bring E about; 0 represents that the causal factor, even if it occurs, does not bring E about. We let C, U, and E be binary variables; $C = 1$ if C occurs, and $C = 0$ otherwise, and analogously with U and E. So $E = 1$ if and only if $q_{ce}C = 1$ or $q_{ue}U = 1$. Taking the probability of both sides, we get (1):[1]

(1) $\mathrm{pr}(E = 1) = \mathrm{pr}(q_{ce}C = 1 \text{ or } q_{ue}U = 1)$

For any propositions A, B, the probability of the proposition that A or B is the probability of A plus the probability of B minus the probability of the proposition that A and B. Hence:

(2) $\mathrm{pr}(E = 1) = \mathrm{pr}(q_{ce}C = 1) + \mathrm{pr}(q_{ue}U = 1) - \mathrm{pr}(q_{ce}q_{ue}CU = 1)$

Now assume that q_{ce}, q_{ue} are jointly independent and also independent of C and of U. Then (2) becomes (3):

(3) $\mathrm{pr}(E = 1) =$
$\quad \mathrm{pr}(q_{ce} = 1) \cdot \mathrm{pr}(C = 1)$
$\quad + \mathrm{pr}(q_{ue} = 1) \cdot \mathrm{pr}(U = 1)$
$\quad - \mathrm{pr}(q_{ce} = 1) \cdot \mathrm{pr}(q_{ue} = 1) \cdot \mathrm{pr}(C = 1, U = 1)$

Hence the probability that $E = 1$, conditional on $C = 1$ and $U = 0$, is as follows:

(4) $\mathrm{pr}(E = 1 \mid C = 1, U = 0) = \mathrm{pr}(q_{ce} = 1)$

This justifies describing $\mathrm{pr}(q_{ce} = 1)$ as the "causal power" (in Cartwright's sense) of C to produce E.

It still remains mysterious how anyone could know—or reasonably estimate—the causal power of C to produce E. But assume that it is known, or believed, that C and U are independent. From (3) and the independence of C and U:

(5) $\mathrm{pr}(E = 1 \mid C = 1) =$
$\quad \mathrm{pr}(q_{ce} = 1)$
$\quad + \mathrm{pr}(q_{ue} = 1) \cdot \mathrm{pr}(U = 1)$
$\quad - \mathrm{pr}(q_{ce} = 1) \cdot \mathrm{pr}(q_{ue} = 1) \cdot \mathrm{pr}(U = 1)$

(6) $\mathrm{pr}(E = 1 \mid C = 0) = \mathrm{pr}(q_{ue} = 1) \cdot \mathrm{pr}(U = 1)$

Noting that the difference of (5) and (6) is $\Delta P_{CE} = \mathrm{pr}(E = 1 \mid C = 1) - \mathrm{pr}(E = 1 \mid C = 0)$, we have (7):

(7) $\Delta P_{CE} = \mathrm{pr}(q_{ce} = 1)$
$$+ \mathrm{pr}(q_{ue} = 1) \cdot \mathrm{pr}(U = 1)$$
$$- \mathrm{pr}(q_{ce} = 1) \cdot \mathrm{pr}(q_{ue} = 1) \cdot \mathrm{pr}(U = 1)$$
$$- \mathrm{pr}(q_{ue} = 1) \cdot \mathrm{pr}(U = 1)$$
$$= \mathrm{pr}(q_{ce} = 1)[1 - \mathrm{pr}(q_{ue} = 1) \cdot \mathrm{pr}(U = 1)]$$

Hence,

(8) $$\frac{\Delta P_{CE}}{[1 - \mathrm{pr}(q_{ue} = 1) \cdot \mathrm{pr}(U = 1)]} = \mathrm{pr}(q_{ce} = 1)$$

Finally, we note that $\mathrm{pr}(q_{ue} = 1) \cdot \mathrm{pr}(U = 1)$ is just the probability that $E = 1$, given that $C = 0$. And so, finally,

(9) $$\frac{\Delta P_{CE}}{[1 - \mathrm{pr}(E = 1 \mid C = 0)]} = \mathrm{pr}(q_{ce} = 1)$$

Equation (9) implies that under the specified assumptions, the causal power of C to generate E can be estimated from ΔP and from the probability that E occurs given that C does not occur, which can all be estimated from observations of C and E alone. Moreover, under otherwise similar assumptions, we obtain the same result no matter how many unobserved causes there are, so long as they are all generative and independent of C. We note for later use that a derivation resulting in an equivalent equation for the causal power of C similar to (9) is possible if there is another (or several) observed causal factor D, independent of C, and we condition on the absence of D.

This transformation of metaphysics into testable mathematics predicts the following for appropriate contexts:

• There should be pairs of cases in which people judge causal powers to be unequal but judge the ΔPs to be equal.
• When an effect always occurs in the absence of a causal factor, rather than judging the factor to have no influence, people should be unwilling to judge the power of the factor to produce the effect.
• When the effect never occurs in the absence of a causal factor, people should judge the efficacy of the factor by ΔP.

Cheng provides experimental evidence that all three are true for contexts to which her theory applies: causal factors that have but two values, present or absent, are all generative and independent.

7.3   Preventive Causes

Now suppose that all unobserved causes U of E are generating, and there is an observed candidate preventing cause F of E. In this case, E will occur if U occurs, U acts to bring E about, and F does not prevent E from occurring:

$$E = q_{ue}U \cdot (1 - q_{fe}F)$$

Cheng's equation is (10):

(10) $\mathrm{pr}(E = 1) = \mathrm{pr}(q_{ue}U \cdot (1 - q_{fe}F) = 1)$

By using (10), we compute that $\mathrm{pr}(q_{ue}U = 1) = \mathrm{pr}(E = 1 \mid F = 0)$, and $\mathrm{pr}(E=1 \mid F=1)=\mathrm{pr}(q_{ue}U=1)\cdot\mathrm{pr}(q_{fe}=0)=\mathrm{pr}(q_{ue}U=1)\cdot(1-\mathrm{pr}(q_{fe}=1))$. We can therefore substitute $\mathrm{pr}(E = 1 \mid F = 0)$ for $\mathrm{pr}(q_{ue}U = 1)$ in the equation for $\mathrm{pr}(E = 1 \mid F = 1)$ and solve for $\mathrm{pr}(q_{fe} = 1)$. The result is (11):

(11) $\mathrm{pr}(q_{fe} = 1) = -\Delta P_f / \mathrm{pr}(E = 1 \mid F = 0)$

Cheng's account of preventive power predicts that in appropriate contexts, if an effect never occurs even when a potential preventive cause is absent, people will be uncertain as to the preventive power, because it is undefined. She reports experiments confirming that prediction.

As Cheng notes, the ceiling effects that follow from her model are standard pieces of experimental practice. If you set out to test a new antibiotic and you apply it to a culture and do not apply it to a control culture and all of the cells in both cultures die, you don't—or shouldn't—conclude that your antibiotic has no effect. Instead, you conclude that the experiment is no good, because, in all probability, some unknown factor independently killed the cultures.

7.4   Generative Interaction

Many, perhaps most, everyday causal relations provide apparent counterexamples to Cheng's theory. Consider the house-current circuit breaker, a lamp switch, and the light on a lamp. The light is on if and only if both the circuit breaker and the lamp switch are on. Suppose that the state of the circuit breaker and the state of the lamp switch are independent, and each is on half the time. If we apply Cheng's formula (9), the causal power of the circuit breaker is

$$\frac{\mathrm{pr}(L = \mathrm{on}\,|\,C = \mathrm{on}) - \mathrm{pr}(L = \mathrm{on}\,|\,C = \mathrm{off})}{1 - \mathrm{pr}(L = \mathrm{on}\,|\,C = \mathrm{off})} = 1/2$$

and the causal power of the lamp switch is also $1/2$. Allan's measure, ΔP, gives the same values. The Rescorla-Wagner equilibrium associative strengths are both $1/2$ when $\beta_1 = \beta_2$. Spellman's measures, ΔP conditional on values of other potential causes, make both causal powers 1 if we condition on the presence of the other variable, and 0 if we condition on the absence of the other variable. And that presents a difficulty for Cheng's theory as well as for Spellman's.

On Cartwright's view, and Cheng's, causal power is supposed to a fundamental feature of the relation between a potential cause and an effect, insensitive to background conditions. But if the circuit breaker is always on, then Cheng's measure of the causal power of the lamp switch is no longer $1/2$, but 1.

Some account of interaction is required, and in collaboration with Laura Novick, Cheng (1999) has provided one. It is based on a simple and compelling intuition: If causes A and B of effect E do not interact, then the set of cases that would exhibit E if exposed to both A and B is the union of the set of cases that would exhibit E if exposed to A alone and the set of cases that would exhibit E if exposed to B alone. If we find otherwise, as in the light and the circuit breaker, then there is an interaction. When A and B are generative and they interact generatively, the explicit mathematical model is (12):

(12) $E = q_{ue}U \oplus q_{ae}A \oplus q_{be}B \oplus q_{ab}AB$

Here $\oplus$ is Boolean addition and $q_{ab} = 1$ represents the proposition that A and B, if both occur, interact to cause E. The probability that $E = 1$ is found by taking the probability that the right hand side of (12) equals 1. As before, we assume that A, B, U, and all of the parameters are independent in probability. The problem is how to use (12) and the independence assumptions to compute the causal power of the interaction, that is, $\mathrm{pr}(q_{ab} = 1)$. (Results equivalent to all of those in this section are in Cheng and Novick (1999).)

When B is absent, the interaction term vanishes, and (12) reduces to (13):

(13) $E = q_{ue}U \oplus q_{ae}A$

Analogously for B when A is absent:

(14) $E = q_{ue}U \oplus q_{be}B$

So the simple causal powers of A and of B, that is, $\mathrm{pr}(q_{ae} = 1)$ and $\mathrm{pr}(q_{be} = 1)$, can be estimated as described in section 7.2, but here we condition on the absence of B to estimate the causal power of A, and condition on the absence of A to estimate the causal power of B. Further, when A or B are both absent:

(15) $E = q_{ue}U$

So the probability that E is produced by unobserved causes, $\mathrm{pr}(q_{ue}U = 1)$, can be estimated.

Because of the independence assumptions, equations (13), (14), and (15) give us all of the terms that occur when the probability of the right-hand side of (12) is taken, except for the causal power of the interaction, $\mathrm{pr}(q_{ab} = 1)$. Substituting in the results of (13), (14), and (15) in the expression for the probability of right-hand side of equation (12), we can then solve for $\mathrm{pr}(q_{ab} = 1)$ from the probability of E when A and B are both present. The result has a simple form if we first define the (counterfactual) probability that E would have, given A and B, if there were no interaction, that is:

(16) $\mathrm{pr}_{\mathrm{NI}}(E = 1 \,|\, A = 1, B = 1) =$
$$\mathrm{pr}(q_{ue}U = 1)$$
$$+\, \mathrm{pr}(q_{ae} = 1)$$
$$+\, \mathrm{pr}(q_{be} = 1)$$
$$-\, \mathrm{pr}(q_{ue}U = 1) \cdot \mathrm{pr}(q_{ae} = 1)$$
$$-\, \mathrm{pr}(q_{ue}U = 1) \cdot \mathrm{pr}(q_{be} = 1)$$
$$-\, \mathrm{pr}(q_{ae} = 1) \cdot \mathrm{pr}(A = 1) \cdot \mathrm{pr}(q_{be} = 1)$$
$$+\, \mathrm{pr}(q_{ue}U = 1) \cdot \mathrm{pr}(q_{ae} = 1) \cdot \mathrm{pr}(q_{be} = 1)$$

We have already shown in equations (13), (14), and (15) how to estimate all quantities on the right-hand side of equation (16). The causal power of the interaction then takes the form of (17):

(17) $\mathrm{pr}(q_{ab} = 1) = \dfrac{\mathrm{pr}(E = 1 \,|\, A = 1, B = 1) - \mathrm{pr}_{\mathrm{NI}}(E = 1 \,|\, A = 1, B = 1)}{1 - \mathrm{pr}_{\mathrm{NI}}(E = 1 \,|\, A = 1, B = 1)}$

This is analogous to Cheng's formula (9) for estimating simple generative causal power.

The Cheng and Novick interaction formula gives a principled account of generative interaction and how to estimate it in the simple case we have considered of two direct, independent, generative causes. The theory gives an intuitive result for the example with which I began, the light, lamp switch, and circuit breaker. In that case the effect is the product of the causes, understood as $(0, 1)$ valued variables, and while the simple causal powers are zero, the interactive causal power of the lamp switch and circuit breaker to turn the light on has the value 1. Further, the theory gives different results from those of a variety of measures of interaction proposed in epidemiology and from the measures of interaction used in standard statistical categorical data analysis. Cheng and Novick consider five other combinations of generative and preventing simple and interactive causes. I will not review them here.

7.5   Cheng Models as Bayes Nets

Cheng and Cheng and Novick are concerned both about how people conceive causal relations and about how they do, or could, discover and use causal relations according to that conception. They give us an answer for a family of cases, those for which we partially know the causal graph (we know which variables are potential causes of others, and we know that some causal connections do not obtain, that there is no confounding, and that there is no association between the effect and potential causes due to unobserved causes) but we do not know the values of the parameters—the causal powers. The aim in these cases is to estimate the causal power of a direct (adjacent) cause of an effect. For noninteracting causes, we can summarize the estimation theory for these circumstances as follows. I assume that the probabilities of any unobserved causes and the probabilities of their causal powers are not zero.

1. Assume that E has a single observed, generating cause A, and a probability-wise independent unobserved preventing cause U. Then the causal power of A to generate E cannot be estimated.

2. Assume that E has one or more observed, generating causes A, B, etc.; zero or more observed preventing causes; and an independent unobserved preventing cause U. Then the ratios of the causal powers of each of the generating causes to one another can be estimated.

3. Assume that *E* has one or more observed, generating causes *A*, *B*, etc.; zero or more observed, preventing causes *C*; and an independent unobserved preventing cause. Then the causal power of each observed preventing cause can be estimated.

4. Assume that *E* has zero or more observed, generating causes *A*, *B*, etc.; zero or more observed preventing causes *C*; and an independent, unobserved generating cause. Then the causal powers of each of the observed causes can be estimated.

5. Assume that *E* has zero or more observed, generating causes *A*, *B*, etc.; any number of observed preventing causes *C*; and an unobserved generating cause *U*. If *U* is not a cause of *A* and no other observed cause *D* of *E* is both an effect of *U* and either an effect of *A* or an effect of another common unobserved cause of *A* and *D*, then the causal power of *A* can be estimated.

From a Bayes net perspective, Cheng's analyses have so far been confined to a comparatively simple family of graphs in which each candidate cause has either a direct influence or no influence on the effect variable. But these are special cases, with special graphs. Causes of an effect can also influence other causes of the same effect, and a cause can be indirect rather than direct. Unobserved common causes too may act in these circumstances. Cheng's theory naturally extends to causal structures represented by more complex directed acyclic graphs, but the extension raises issues, specifically, what does the "causal power" of one variable to generate or prevent another correspond to in parameterizations of such graphs, and when can such causal powers be estimated from observations? Those are the issues of the remainder of this chapter.

Estimating the simple total causal power given the true causal graph
Consider the structure in figure 7.1, where *W*, *U* are unobserved and independent. Consider the case where there is no interaction and all causes are generative. The graph in figure 7.1 then corresponds to the following equations:

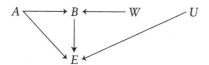

Figure 7.1

$$E = q_{ue}U \oplus q_{be}B \oplus q_{ae}A$$

$$B = q_{wb}W \oplus q_{ab}A$$

Cheng's methods (1997)—essentially those of sections 7.2, 7.3—apply to this case. In this case, to estimate q_{be} it is essential, not optional, to condition on the absence of A, and similarly on the absence of B to estimate q_{ae}. But the "simple causal power" of A is now ambiguous: it can mean the causal power of A associated with the $A \rightarrow E$ edge alone, which is the probability of E given A and the absence of all other causes of E (B and W and U in this case), or it can mean the causal power of A associated with the $A \rightarrow E$ edge and the $A \rightarrow B \rightarrow E$ path, which is the probability of E given A and the absence of all other causes of E that are not effects of A (W and U in this case). I will call the former quantity the *direct causal power* of A, and when the probability is greater than 0 that E occurs given that A occurs and that no other causes of E, other than effects of A, occur, I will call the latter quantity the *total causal power* of A. Given a directed graph, the set of all the direct causal powers somehow determines the total causal powers. How?

Consider a more complicated example (figure 7.2). Suppose that D is a preventive cause of E, that A is a preventive cause of G, and that all other causes are generative, and suppose that all of the q parameters are known, except for those associated with R, S, T, W, V, and U, which are unobserved variables. In symbols:

$$E = (q_{ue}U \oplus q_{ce}C \oplus q_{fe}F \oplus q_{ge}G)(1 - q_{de}D)$$

$$C = q_{bc}B \oplus q_{wc}W$$

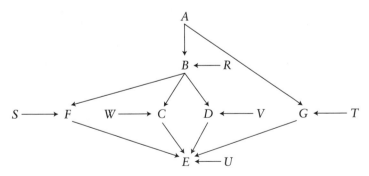

Figure 7.2

$D = q_{bd}B \oplus q_{vc}V$

$F = q_{bf}B \oplus q_{sf}S$

$G = q_{tg}T(1 - q_{ag}A)$

$B = q_{ab}A \oplus qrbR$

Substituting, we get (21):

(21) $\quad E = (q_{ue}U \oplus q_{ge}q_{tg}T(1 - q_{ag}A) \oplus q_{ce}(q_{bc}(q_{ab}A \oplus q_{rb}R) \oplus q_{wc}W)$
$\oplus q_{fe}(q_{bf}(q_{ab}A \oplus q_{rb}R) \oplus q_{sf}))$
$\cdot (1 - q_{de}(q_{bd}(q_{ab}A \oplus q_{rb}R) \oplus q_{vc}V))$

Hence the total causal power of A to generate E is given by (22):

(22) $\quad \mathrm{pr}(E = 1 \,|\, A = 1, U = 0, R = 0, W = 0, V = 0, S = 0) =$
$\mathrm{pr}(q_{ab} = 1)$
$\cdot [\mathrm{pr}(q_{bc} = 1) \cdot \mathrm{pr}(q_{ce} = 1) + \mathrm{pr}(q_{bf} = 1) \cdot \mathrm{pr}(q_{fe} = 1)]$
$\cdot [1 - \mathrm{pr}(q_{ab} = 1) \cdot \mathrm{pr}(q_{bd} = 1) \cdot \mathrm{pr}(q_{de} = 1)]$

Estimating causal powers when there are unobserved confounders
All of the procedures so far assume that there is no unobserved common cause influencing the cause of an effect and the effect itself. But if the causal graph is known, direct and total causal powers can sometimes be estimated even when there is such confounding.

Consider the simple case of figure 7.3, where U is unobserved and generative. The total causal power of A to generate E can be estimated by the method of the previous subsection from $\mathrm{pr}(q_{be} = 1)$. The causal power of B cannot be estimated by any of the methods so far described. But it can be estimated. If all causes are generative:

$E = q_{be}B \oplus q_{ue}U$

$B = q_{ab}A \oplus q_{ub}U$

Substituting and factoring, we get the following:

$E = q_{be}q_{ab}A \oplus (q_{be}q_{ub} \oplus q_{ue})U$

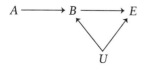

Figure 7.3

Now $\text{pr}(q_{be} = 1) \cdot \text{pr}(q_{ab} = 1)$ can be estimated by the methods of section 7.2. But A and B are unconfounded, and so $\text{pr}(q_{ab} = 1)$ can be estimated analogously. The ratio gives $\text{pr}(q_{be} = 1)$. It can be shown that knowledge of $\text{pr}(q_{be} = 1)$ permits the calculation of the probability of E given an intervention that fixes (or randomly assigns a value to) B.

The technique, called in econometrics the method of instrumental variables, need not work for other parametrizations of structures with binary variables. I believe it does not work if A is generative and B preventing, or if A is preventing and B generative, or if both A and B are preventing, although I have not proved as much. Noisy OR gates have other similarities to linear models: in both linear and noisy-OR-gate models the Tetrad Representation Theorem (Spirtes et al. 1993, 2001) provides both a graphical condition and a relation among measured correlations sufficient for four measured variables to have a single unmeasured common cause.

Consider next the case where all causes are generative and U and W are not observed (figure 7.4). The direct causal power of A to generate B and of B to generate E can be estimated; more surprisingly, so can the total causal power of A to generate E. To estimate $\text{pr}(q_{be} = 1)$, condition on the absence of A and apply the method of section 7.2. To estimate $\text{pr}(q_{ab} = 1)$, apply the method of section 7.2 directly, since there is no confounding. Now by an obvious variant of previous results, the total causal power of A to generate E is $\text{pr}(q_{ab} = 1) \cdot \text{pr}(q_{be} = 1)$.

Finally, consider a circumstance that sometimes arises in science, and presumably in everyday life as well, in which the effect itself influences what is observed. Let "S" represent the property that a system is observed, and suppose that the causal structure is that given in figure 7.5.

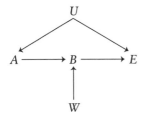

Figure 7.4

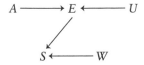

Figure 7.5

All of the observations are conditioned on $S = 1$, and U and W are unobserved. In this case the probability that $q_{ae} = 1$ cannot be estimated. Recall from the Monte Hall problem, described in chapter 6, that, conditional on their common effect, two otherwise independent variables, in this case A and U, are dependent. So A and U are dependent conditional on E. But the same is true if the conditioning variable is any *descendant* of a common effect (Pearl 1988). So A and U are dependent conditional on S.

7.6   Discovering the Causal Graph

The theory of estimation for Cheng models so far developed assumes that the causal graph is completely known, save that if the associated direct causal powers are zero, some represented edges may be phantoms. My separation of causal graphs and estimates of causal powers may seem artificial and unmotivated. Since the occurrences of features we encounter in life are usually ordered by their known time of occurrence, given a set of features whose causal relations are to be investigated, why not apply Cheng's method, the method of sections 7.2 and 7.3, to determine the influence of each feature on subsequent features? The method is formally a sequence of regressions: in judging the influence, or causal power, of a candidate cause, all other observed candidate causes are conditioned on. Then the causal graph would appear to emerge as a result of, not a precondition for, the estimation of causal powers.

The preceding section and the preceding chapter supply an obvious reason why the method will not be reliable: unobserved common causes. We have seen that the estimation methods of sections 7.2 and 7.3 are generally insufficient when there are unobserved common causes at work, and often we have no idea before we begin inquiry whether such factors are operating.

In the last decade there has been extensive research into the causal information that can and cannot be obtained under the Markov and faithfulness assumptions, or similar conditions, and it continues. I will not survey it here (see Spirtes et al. 2001, especially chapter 12, for a review), but I will give some examples.

Suppose, to take almost the worst case, that time order is not known and nothing is known about the true causal structure, except that there is one, and that the Markov and faithfulness assumptions hold. Our aim is to estimate the causal power of A to influence E. Suppose that the true unknown structure is that given in figure 7.6 and that only C, D, A, and E are observed. Figure 7.6 implies that C and D are independent of each other and independent of E conditional on A, and that no other observed independencies hold. We can begin the inquiry by supposing that for all we know, any of C, D, A, E may be directly dependent on one another (figure 7.7). Examining figure 7.6, we see that C and D are independent, and so there can be no direct connection between them (figure 7.8). But C is independent of E conditional on A, and D is also independent of E conditional on A. Hence there can be no direct connection between C and E or between D and E (figure 7.9). Since C and D are independent, but not independent conditional on A, it follows from the faithfulness assumption that they must have arrows directed into A, although one cannot tell whether they cause A or have a common cause with A or

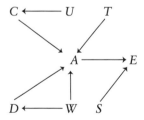

Figure 7.6

Figure 7.7

both (figure 7.10). (In figure 7.10 the small circles mean that we cannot tell whether there is a direct cause, an unobserved common cause, or both.) Now C and D are jointly independent of E conditional on A, but neither is independent of E. If E caused A, then C and D would be independent of E, and they are not. If there were in addition an unobserved common cause of E, then C and D would not be independent of E conditional on A (Monte Hall again). So we conclude that the causal structure is that of figure 7.11, and the causal power of A to generate (or prevent) E can therefore be estimated by the methods of section 7.2. For the general algorithm and proofs that it gives the correct result under the Markov and faithfulness conditions, as well as other procedures for learning Bayes nets from data, see Spirtes et al. 2001.

Figure 7.8

Figure 7.9

Figure 7.10

Figure 7.11

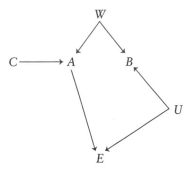

Figure 7.12

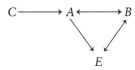

Figure 7.13

Finally, consider a case in which the time order is known and a causal power can be estimated, but not by a regression procedure. Suppose that the true causal structure is that given in figure 7.12, with U and W unobserved. Estimating the causal power of A by conditioning on B or on the absence of B will result in the wrong answer (Monte Hall yet again). But an elaboration of the procedure illustrated previously results in the structure in figure 7.13, where the double headed arrow indicates the presence of an unobserved common cause. The causal power of A can then be estimated by the method of section 7.2, except that we do not condition on B.

7.7   Conclusion

Some of the results of section 7.5 suggest experiments on human subjects, whether adults or children, that have not been done, and some of which should be. The normative theory, Cheng's theory embedded in causal Bayes nets, may of course not describe human judgement precisely. It may be, for example, that people typically ignore the possibility of unobserved common causes and repair their erroneous judgements only as it proves necessary, and, of course, there are memory and processing limitations. For that reason Cheng's recent study (1999) of the under- and overestimates that result from incorrect assumptions is an especially valuable step. We need, besides, an understanding of how incorrect causal Bayes nets—networks that postulate connections that don't exist, networks that omit common causes, networks that leave out connections that do exist—can be remedied without starting over from scratch. Most of the data from which an erroneous network has been learned will have long since been forgotten when new phenomena are discovered that require its modification. Neural-net models, for example, typically must be retrained when a new property is considered, and that is a feature very much to be avoided in a psychological model. There is as yet no repair theory for Bayes nets that is compatible with severe memory and computational limitations. In the next chapter, however, I consider some interactions between causal Bayes-net representations and memory and computational limitations.

8

Learning Procedures

8.1 Introduction: The Virtues of Rescorla-Wagner

Our consideration of child and adult causal judgement has only hinted at learning heuristics for causal Bayes nets. The essential questions— in my view, some of the most important issues about human learning— concern the algorithmic procedures people, especially young people, carry out in naive causal learning, where "naive" means at least before any statistics is taught. This chapter reviews some of the theoretical possibilities and their advantages and disadvantages. I begin with a theory that appears not to be empirically adequate for the psychology of causal learning, the Rescorla-Wagner model, but which has striking virtues one or another of which other theoretical alternatives so far lack.

The Rescorla-Wagner model of classical conditioning has several signal advantages, both as a plausible theory of learning and as a useful working hypothesis. I will list those that seem to me most important:

· Implementing RW requires minimal memory. The learner need only remember a single number for each "cue" under consideration. Past data need not be remembered.

· RW is computationally tractable. The learner need only execute a simple algebraic operation. More technically, the complexity of RW computation is a linear function of the number of cues considered.

· RW gives a theory of learning dynamics. Subject to some empirically determined parameters, RW yields a response curve for the learner that is a unique function of the data presented to the learner and four parameters.

· RW has intelligible asymptotics. In many cases, the equilibrium values of the RW learning function are conditional ΔP values (Cheng 1997).

• The RW model is a pretty good qualitative approximation for lots of learning phenomena.

Nonetheless, RW has some artificial restrictions that a correct learning strategy should generalize. In particular, the RW algorithm presupposes a set of cues and an outcome property, assumes all of these are coded as binary—present or absent—and assumes that their degree, where that makes sense, has no influence on learning. But people discover novel properties and investigate their causal relations, and sometimes matters of degree do matter to some degree.

Some of the alternative learning strategies that are prominent in the psychological or Bayes-net literatures are these:

• *Data-driven point estimates of causal strength* Cheng's model is of this kind: subjects estimate causal strength from observations, and a potential cause is held to be actual if the estimate is nonzero. One can imagine these procedures as general learning algorithms for which values of variables or features are given and the time order of occurrence of related events is given (potential causes before effects).

• *Adaptive scores for causal models* There are many statistical procedures that assign an initial score to alternative hypotheses—in this case, alternative causal hypotheses—and alter that score by some rule as data are acquired. I refer to all of these as adaptive scores. The best known is Bayesian conditioning, in which an initial or prior probability is assigned to all conceivably relevant alternative hypotheses and for each hypothesis a probability (called a likelihood) is assigned to all finite sequences of data. When a new datum is received, the probability of each hypothesis is changed to its conditional probability, given the new datum. Typically, the likelihoods do not change with the data.

• *Model construction from constraint detection* Constraint-detection algorithms apply some statistical procedure or other to identify (or at least guess) patterns in the data and then use the patterns (rather than the data itself) to construct one or more causal explanations, which may contain parameters with unspecified values (e.g., corresponding to "causal strength," etc.). The parameter values may then be separately estimated from the data. Techniques of this kind formed the beginning of psychometrics, and include Spearman's early tetrad analysis and Thurstone's factor analysis, but there are also many other newer and more robust techniques.

I will consider the advantages and disadvantages of each of these strategies as a starting point for developing a theory of human causal learning.

8.2   Point Estimates of Causal Powers

Cheng and her collaborators give formulas for estimating causal powers from joint frequencies of potential causes and their potential effects. The formulas are clearly intended to describe what subjects do after they have observed sufficient data, and no theory is provided for what processing (other than remembering relevant frequencies and conditional frequencies) subjects do in the meanwhile, nor is any explanation given of how sufficiency is determined. The memory and processing requirements for her estimates are not large. Subjects need to remember the relative frequency of an effect conditional on each observed potential cause and the absence of all other causes, and the frequency of each effect in the absence of all of the observed potential causes. Given those numbers, simple algebra suffices.

Besides the absence of a dynamics, several examples in the previous chapter illustrate that there are many circumstances in which causal powers cannot be correctly estimated by these methods, but can nonetheless be correctly estimated.

Cheng and her collaborators have provided a persuasive experimental demonstration of the formation of the selection of novel causal categories from among predicates of varying specificity (e.g., red/blue versus colored/not colored), but a theory of the discovery of causal relations that focuses on estimating causal powers of observed features to produce an observed effect essentially assumes there are no unobserved common causes that contribute to the association of putative causes and their putative effects. In many cases that may be so, but as a model of human learning, it assumes that humans cannot learn that so far unnoticed or unobserved factors are producing associations among observed factors. That too may be so, although I doubt it, but the matter should certainly be tested.

8.3   Adaptive Scores: The Bayesian Way

Rigorous Bayesian methods for learning causal hypotheses assign an initial or prior probability to all alternative causal hypotheses, and also assign prior or initial probabilities to any parameters (e.g., causal strengths, or linear coefficients, or conditional probabilities, etc., depending on the class of models considered). Each causal hypothesis and set of related parameter values determines a probability, or likelihood, for any sequence of data. The total probability of any data sequence is thus the sum, over all models and parameter values, of the probability of the data sequence conditional on the model and parameter values, multiplied by the probability of the model and the parameter values. As each new datum is acquired, the previous probability of each causal model and parameter setting for that model is changed to the conditional probability, on the previous probability measure, of the causal model and parameter setting, given the new datum.

The Bayesian formalism has the advantage that it easily accommodates various ideas about reasoning from evidence that are widely championed. One example is considered in the next chapter. Further, the Bayesian formalism has (or can have) nice memory features. The force of the whole sequence of previous data up to a time is captured by the probability measure at that time; the data themselves do not have to be remembered, only the probability distribution, and for various families of probability distributions, any particular probability measure can be uniquely described by a few numerical parameters.

As an account of human causal learning, however, the Bayesian formalism has some serious difficulties. First, in many cases the apparatus is indifferent to the order in which the data are obtained; the same probability measure results even if the data are permuted. Human learning appears not to work like that. Second, the formalism is computationally intractable. As a consequence, Bayesian statistics has until recently often been a kind of bait and switch enterprise in which alternative hypotheses were severely (and often unjustifiably) restricted at the outset, and posterior probabilities on the evidence were not computed but rather approximated by formulas that hold only in the limit of large samples. Ingenious work in Bayesian statistics in recent years has overcome the latter problem, but only at the price of computationally intensive numerical-simulation methods. The existence of astronomical numbers of possible hypotheses is still a fundamental difficulty for Bayesian data-mining methods, and almost all "Bayesian" algorithms that mine data for causal relations use various heuristics to avoid scoring all possible models. Third, the Bayesian formalism has a problem with novelty: no feasible, consistent Bayesian method for introducing new, unobserved causes of observed associations is known. That is, while a handful of alternative explanations of data may be computed using Bayesian methods even though they contain unobserved common causes (latent variables), no correct, feasible, general Bayesian procedure is known that provides correct information—in the large sample limit—about the existence of unobserved common causes of observed variables.

Much of the appeal of the Bayesian formalism is normative rather than descriptive, and the preponderance of recent psychological work on human judgement under uncertainty assumes that rationality requires coherent degrees of belief and Bayesian updating on evidence. There are theoretical considerations that argue against the Bayesian standard for rationality. Whatever else is true of our notion of rationality, it is limited by these principles:

• To obtain an all-things-considered goal, a rational agent chooses a means that will obtain that goal, if there is such a means.

• An agent is not irrational if she does not do what she cannot do, and is not irrational if she does not try to do what she rationally believes she cannot do.

I assume that our cognitive processes are computationally bounded: insofar as they are discrete, they are Turing computable. I assume that they have low complexity bounds. Insofar as conscious or unconscious computations are nonpolynomial-hard, we do not do them, or do them only in easy cases. On these two assumptions, three theoretical results argue that rationality does not require us, or does not always require us, to be coherent Bayesians:

• If we have probability assignments for sentences over a "rich" language, that is, one adequate for standard first-order logic, we cannot be probabilistically coherent unless we are infinitely dogmatic, that is, unless we assign zero probability to an infinity of contingent propositions. That is an elementary consequence of the undecidability of first-order logic.

• There are discovery problems—specifications of alternative hypotheses and disjoint sets of possible sequences of observations respectively consistent with each alternative hypothesis—for which *no* Turing-computable Bayesian who learns by using the evidence to update a prior probability assignment for the alternatives will reliably converge to the true hypothesis. That is, for each mathematically computable Bayesian method, there will be a hypothesis among the alternatives such that for some data sequence consistent with that hypothesis and only that hypothesis, the Bayesian learner will not converge to assigning probability 1 to that hypothesis. But for some of the same problems, there are Turing computable non-Bayesian learners that do reliably converge to the true hypothesis, no matter which alternative is true (Osherson et al. 1988, Juhl 1997).

• A principled theory for being *approximately* Bayesian is only now beginning to be developed (Schervish et al., forthcoming). While there are measures of "distance" from one probability measure to another, there is no standard measure from nonprobability measures to probability measures, nor is there a comparative measure of which nonprobability measures are more nearly probability measures.

8.4   Building on Patterns in the Data

Constraint detection procedures typically determine that two variables are independent (not associated) or are independent conditional on values of other observed variables. As this information is acquired, the procedures construct features of the world to explain the patterns of dependency and independency. Typically, in the absence of further information (time order, for example) what results is a set of alternative causal models, alternative directed graphs, although with background knowledge a unique explanation may result. Early psychometric algorithms, factor analysis, for example, had a similar overall strategy, but overreached. Unlike factor analysis and the heuristic procedures that preceded it, modern constraint-based algorithms for discovering causal structure have proofs of their large-sample ("pointwise") correctness under quite general assumptions (Spirtes et al. 1993, 2001), have been extensively tested on simulated data, and have generated real, independently established predictions.

The advantages of constraint-detection methods as a model of human causal learning are these: they are computationally tractable when the actual causal relations are sparse, that is, when most features have no causal connection with one another; in some contexts, they permit the discovery of unobserved causes of observed associations; the discovery procedures can be designed so that if they are aborted (for example, because computational demands become to large) the partial information obtained before aborting the procedure is correct; they can make extensive use of previous knowledge of the domain, thereby decreasing complexity of computation and increasing the significant information that can be obtained from observations.

The disadvantage of causal-inference algorithms based on constraint detection is in their memory requirements. Existing algorithms require comparatively large data sets, and they do not reliably build up correct explanations from new data and previous explanations.

8.5   Heuristics and Compromises

Since neither adaptive scores nor existing constraint-based algorithms meet reasonable behavioral constraints, the real issue is which idealization to start from in searching for an empirically adequate—better, *true*—account of human causal learning. In practice, many data-mining algorithms inspired by Bayesian statistics are "greedy": they start with an initial model and iteratively choose whichever small variation of it most increases the probability. The number of "Bayesian" heuristics is limited only by ingenuity. And, of course, there are other kinds of adaptive scores besides posterior probabilities.

Constraint-based algorithms can diminish their data requirements by artificially boosting sample sizes—that is, by treating a sample of 5 as though it were a sample of 50 or 500 for the purpose of deciding whether features are or are not independent or conditionally independent, or by otherwise changing the decision procedure for independence. While such devices sacrifice reliability to reduce uncertainty, they need not alter the large-sample reliabilities of constraint-based algorithms. The problem for such strategies then becomes to form an empirically adequate model of how erroneous conclusions can be correctly identified and modified if most data are forgotten.

Almost finally, the dichotomy between learning algorithms with adaptive scores and learning algorithms based on identifying patterns of constraints in the data is not quite a dichotomy. The two learning strategies can be combined in many ways. One such combination has proved remarkably good. On the most common one tested, data from a large graphical model simulating causal relations among variables in an emergency room, a very accurate greedy procedure due to Christopher Meek uses probabilities, not for individual graphical models, but for

Markov equivalence classes of such models. Despite the greedy heuristic, the procedure is very slow. Its run time is cut in half, without loss of accuracy, if it starts with an initial Markov equivalence class obtained from a constraint-based procedure.

8.6   Building on Sand

The problem of finding a model for causal learning that explains human behavior is made considerably more difficult by the ambiguity of what is to be explained. Typical experimental designs ask subjects to judge "efficacy" or "causal power" or something similar on scales that may vary from −100 to 100 or 0 to 100, or to give a causal explanation. These judgements are the outcome of the treatment (the instructions and data) given to the subject. Very rarely, subjects are required or allowed to manipulate some feature, and that manipulation is the outcome. Data presentations vary enormously, and include presentations of numerical statistics for various properties, graphical presentations (histograms or pie charts), and one-by-one observation of cases. When the subjects observe cases, the number of cases observed by each subject is typically fixed in advance by the experimenter, but may sometimes vary from subject to subject.

Here are some of the issues these experimental designs generate:

1. The responses given in typical learning experiments vary with the format in which the data are presented.

2. Responses to requests for judgements of "efficacy," etc., may be reports of judgements of some measure of causal strength, reports of judgements of subjects' confidence that there is some causal connection, or a mixture of both.

3. Subjects' understanding of the "power" or "efficacy" of A to produce B may be separated from their judgement about what would happen about B if someone were to act to produce A—they may, in other words, be in the grip of a theory about "causation" which biases their verbal responses.

4. Requests for causal explanations are embedded in a complex of conversational conventions, moral attitudes, and other factors not under the experimenter's control.

5. Designs in which subjects observe a fixed number of trials may not be at equilibrium or be "asymptotic" for iterative learning models such as Rescorla-Wagner.

Designs should have an ecological validity, but only for the ecology of what one is trying to get at. If fundamental preverbal or subverbal learning mechanisms are being studied, point 1 argues that data should be presented one by one as observed cases. If, by contrast, the judgements of physicians who see summary data are under study, then numerical formats might be appropriate. The important thing is not to confuse one ecology with another, for example, not to argue that people do not learn from covariation, because when asked to explain morally laden cases, they do not seek out covariation data.

Because of points 2, 3, and 4, investigations of fundamental human causal learning might be designed to have outcomes that are nonverbal attempts at problem solutions, for example, a choice of optional routes to try to bring about some state of affairs. And because of point 5, data that are relevant to many theoretical issues must let the subjects themselves determine when they have seen enough evidence. Experiments on causal judgement that satisfy these various strictures seem to be rather rare. Even then, there are difficulties. Danks (2001) points out that even in the simple case of two generative, unconfounded, noninteracting causes C_1 and C_2 of an effect E, there are probabilities where C_1 has greater causal power and larger conditional ΔP than C_2, but the probability of E occurring on an intervention to make C_2 present is greater than the probability of E on an intervention to make C_1 present.

9

Representation and Rationality: The Case of Backward Blocking

9.1 Backward Blocking

One of Isaac Newton's Rules of Reasoning in Natural Philosophy, the *Vera Causa* rule in book 3 of *Principia*, recommends this: postulate no more causes except as are true and sufficient to save the phenomena. Newton intended the rule to justify assuming that only the force of gravitation acts on the planets and their satellites, and on the tides, for he had established that cause, and it sufficed.

Some recent work on associative learning (Van Hamme et al. 1994) argues that adults sometimes apply a version of the *Vera Causa* rule in contexts with less *gravitas*. In "cue competition" or "backward blocking," features *A* and *B* appear together followed by an effect *E*, and judgements of the "efficacy" of both *A* and *B* increase. If *A* then appears alone and is followed by *E*, the judgement of the efficacy of *B* is reduced. The causal role of *A* is established and suffices to explain the data.

It is well known that backward blocking is inconsistent with the familiar Rescorla-Wagner model of associative learning, and various modifications of the model have been proposed to deal with the phenomenon. But backward blocking has also been explained by various ad hoc causal models. Using causal graphical models, predictions about backward blocking and about many related experiments can be uniformly derived from alternative causal theories, and for simple experiments the possible theories and their predictions can be classified. Extending the classification to more complex experiments takes us into open mathematical problems in the theory of Bayes nets.

9.2   Experiments

We consider experiments in which there are three trials involving three variables, potential causes A and B and effect E. In each of the first two trials the experimenter forces each potential cause, A and B, to be present or absent, and the subject observes these actions. The subject also observes, sequentially, the value of E on the first and second trials and is told in advance of all trials what the values of A and B will be (i.e., present or absent) on the third trial. The subject is required, after each of the first two trials, to judge the probability that E will occur on the third trial. A variation also elicits from the subject a probability for E in the condition of the third trial before any trials are carried out. In either variation, if we ignore the cases in which neither A nor B are present, there are 108 possible experiments of this kind; allowing such cases, there are 256 experiments.

I will be particularly concerned with the experiment: $\langle A, B, E;$ $A, \sim B, E; \sim A, B, \_\rangle$, where "$\sim$" indicates that the cause operated on is not present. Indicating trial numbers by subscripts, I will say that *backward blocking* occurs if and only if in this experiment subjects' judgements of probability satisfy (1):

(1) $\mathrm{pr}(E_3 \mid E_1) > \mathrm{pr}(E_3 \mid E_1, E_2)$

This formulation does not prejudice the analysis for or against any particular causal theory of subjects' judgements.

9.3   Backward Blocking Does Not Hold in All Models

There are six parameters whose joint values characterize all possible joint probability distributions on A, B, E that satisfy the Markov Assumption for the following graph:

They are:

$$Q_A = \text{pr}(A = 1)$$

$$Q_B = \text{pr}(B = 1)$$

$$Q_{AB} = \text{pr}(E = 1 \mid A = 1, B = 1)$$

$$Q_{A \sim B} = \text{pr}(E = 1 \mid A = 1, B = 0)$$

$$Q_{\sim AB} = \text{pr}(E = 1 \mid A = 0, B = 1)$$

$$Q_{\sim A \sim B} = \text{pr}(E = 1 \mid A = 0, B = 0)$$

In the experiment we are considering, on trial 1, A and B are forced to be present; on trial 2, A is forced to be present, and B is prevented from being present; on trial 3, B is forced to be present, and A is is prevented from being present. Hence the Q values for A and for B are known and fixed for each trial. Consider a prior subjective probability distribution $\text{pr}(Q_{AB}, Q_{A \sim B}, Q_{\sim AB}, Q_{\sim A \sim B})$ for which the Qs are all independent. Implicitly conditioning on the values forced on A and B, we find that the joint prior subjective probability for the effects is the following:

$$\text{pr}(E_1 = 1, E_2 = 1, E_3 = 1)$$

$$= \iiint Q_{AB} \, \text{pr}(Q_{AB}) Q_{A \sim B} \, \text{pr}(Q_{A \sim B}) Q_{\sim AB} \, \text{pr}(Q_{\sim AB})$$

$$\times \, dQ_{AB} \, dQ_{A \sim B} \, dQ_{\sim AB}$$

$$= \int Q_{AB} \, \text{pr}(Q_{AB}) \, dQ_{AB} \int Q_{A \sim B} \, \text{pr}(Q_{A \sim B}) \, dQ_{A \sim B}$$

$$\times \int Q_{\sim AB} \, \text{pr}(Q_{\sim AB}) \, dQ_{\sim AB}$$

The marginal probabilities and relevant conditional probabilities over $E_1 = 1$, $E_2 = 1$, $E_3 = 1$ are these:

$$\text{pr}(E_1 = 1) = \int Q_{AB} \, \text{pr}(Q_{AB}) \, dQ_{AB}$$

$$\text{pr}(E_2 = 1) = \int Q_{A \sim B} \, \text{pr}(Q_{A \sim B}) \, dQ_{A \sim B}$$

$$\text{pr}(E_3 = 1) = \int Q_{\sim AB} \, \text{pr}(Q_{\sim AB}) \, dQ_{\sim AB}$$

$$\text{pr}(E_1 = 1, E_3 = 1) = \int Q_{AB} \, \text{pr}(Q_{AB}) \, dQ_{AB} \int Q_{\sim AB} \, \text{pr}(Q_{\sim AB}) \, dQ_{\sim AB}$$

$$\text{pr}(E_1 = 1, E_2 = 1) = \int Q_{AB} \, \text{pr}(Q_{AB}) \, dQ_{AB} \int Q_{A \sim B} \, \text{pr}(Q_{A \sim B}) \, dQ_{A \sim B}$$

Since

$$\mathrm{pr}(E_3 = 1 \mid E_1 = 1) = \mathrm{pr}(E_1 = 1, E_3 = 1)/\mathrm{pr}(E_1 = 1)$$

and

$$\mathrm{pr}(E_3 = 1 \mid E_1 = 1, E_2 = 1)$$
$$= \mathrm{pr}(E_1 = 1, E_2 = 1, E_3 = 1)/\mathrm{pr}(E_1 = 1, E_2 = 1)$$

it follows that

$$\mathrm{pr}(E_3 = 1) = \mathrm{pr}(E_3 = 1 \mid E_1 = 1) = \mathrm{pr}(E_3 = 1 \mid E_1 = 1, E_2 = 1)$$

and backward blocking does not hold.

It will help for subsequent analysis if we represent this model graphically. A well-known trick in the Bayes-net literature is to expand a causal graph by introducing new vertices representing the independent parameters of a model and new edges from these new vertices to the effects that the parameters control. The Markov Assumption and its consequences (the d-separation algorithm) then determine the conditional dependencies and independencies. One graphical representation of the model above is the following graph with three disconnected pieces:

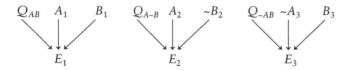

(Here I have taken the innocuous liberty of indicating the values of the A and B variables in the vertices corresponding to the three trials.) The Markov Assumption implies that, conditional on its parents in the graph, E_3 is independent of E_2, and of E_1 and E_2 jointly, that is, conditional on the value of $Q_{A \sim B}$ and on $\sim A_3$ and B_3. These vertices, in turn, have no parents in the graph, and so are independent of everything except E_3. Hence, there is no backward blocking.

9.4   Backward Blocking Holds for Cheng Models

Backward blocking will hold if we impose some appropriate dependence among the Q parameters. For generative, noninteractive Cheng models with no unobserved causes, we have (2):

(2) $E = q_{AE}A \vee q_{BE}B$

Here "$\vee$" is inclusive "or." Further, for the Cheng model, for any trial:

$$Q_{AB} = Q_{A \sim B} + Q_{\sim AB} - Q_{A \sim B}Q_{\sim AB}$$

$$Q_{A \sim B} = \mathrm{pr}(E = 1 \mid A = 1, B = 0) = \mathrm{pr}(q_{AE} = 1)$$

$$Q_{\sim AB} = \mathrm{pr}(E = 1 \mid A = 0, B = 1) = \mathrm{pr}(q_{BE} = 1)$$

$$Q_{\sim A \sim B} = \mathrm{pr}(E = 1 \mid A = 0, B = 0) = 0$$

Rather than attempt to derive backward blocking by disentangling integrals for the Cheng model, we can use a graphical representation of the model and a consequence of the Markov Assumption and the faithfulness assumption to see that $\mathrm{pr}(E_3 \mid E_2, E_1)$ is not equal to $\mathrm{pr}(E_3 \mid E_1)$. The graphical representation of the Cheng model is this:

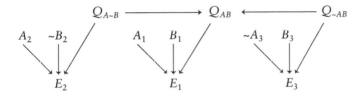

The arrows between the Q vertices are necessary because Cheng's generative model takes the causal power of A and B together to be a (positive) function of the causal power of A and the causal power of B, in agreement with equation (2).

Now we have a Bayes net and inferences that involve the collider phenomenon, roughly analogous to the Monte Hall game and to Pearl's example of the relations between a car starting, the state of its fuel supply, and the state of its battery. In the Cheng model, $Q_{A \sim B}$ and $Q_{\sim AB}$ are independent, as are E_2 and E_3. E_1 is a descendant of both $Q_{A \sim B}$ and $Q_{\sim AB}$. *Conditional on* E_1, $Q_{A \sim B}$ and $Q_{\sim AB}$ are no longer independent. And because E_2 is a descendant of $Q_{A \sim B}$ and E_3 is a descendant of $Q_{\sim AB}$, E_3 and E_2 are likewise no longer independent, conditional on E_1. Hence, $\mathrm{pr}(E_3 \mid E_2, E_1)$ is not equal to $\mathrm{pr}(E_3 \mid E_1)$. The inequality does not itself establish backward blocking, because it does not say which conditional probability, $\mathrm{pr}(E_3 \mid E_2, E_1)$ or $\mathrm{pr}(E_3 \mid E_1)$, is greater. For that, we need another consideration.

Rather than considering the continuous quantities Q_{AB}, $Q_{A \sim B}$, and $Q_{\sim AB}$, I will replace them with the binary variables Y, Z, and X, respectively. We then have a noisy OR gate in which Z and only Z generates E_2 with probability $\mathrm{pr}(q_{ze_2} = 1)$, Y and only Y generates E_1 with probability $\mathrm{pr}(q_{ye_1} = 1)$, and X and only X generates E_3 with probability $\mathrm{pr}(q_{xe_3} = 1)$, and further, X and Z generate Y by analogy with equation (2) above. Some tedious algebra (which, along with much else, I owe to Peter Spirtes) shows that in this case $\mathrm{pr}(E_3 \,|\, E_1) \geq \mathrm{pr}(E_3 \,|\, E_1, E_2)$. I believe, but have not proved, the same result holds for probabilities computed with any prior probability distribution over the Q variables that is faithful to their relations in figure 9.3. For any noisy OR gate $Z \to Y \gets X$, the probability of X conditional on Y is greater than the probability of X conditional on Y and Z, and the same is true if, as in this case, we consider the probability of E_3, the effect of X, conditional on the respective effects of Y and of Y and Z. Pearl (1988) calls this phenomenon "explaining away." It is an essential feature of the noisy OR gate parameterization; the reverse inequality would hold, for example, if we had the same graph but $Y = q_{zxy} \cdot Z \cdot X$, as in the interaction case discussed in chapter 7.

9.5   General Considerations

We can describe a large class of theories of causal judgement in experiments of the kind considered here by the graphical structures imposed on the Q parameters and the functional relations among the variables. Cheng's model imposes one particular graphical structure on the Q parameters, but there are 25 distinct possible directed acyclic graphs on the three Q vertices. As noted in an earlier chapter, the 25 graphs on 3 vertices form 11 classes of graphs such that all and only the graphs in the same class are Markov equivalent, that is, imply the same set of independencies and conditional independencies. Graphs in different Markov equivalence classes will imply different sets of independence and conditional-independence relations among the Q variables. These independencies (but not necessarily the conditional independencies) between Q variables are reflected in independencies between the corresponding E variables. Many of these theories may be empirically uninteresting, but few of them have been investigated either theoretically or experimentally. The same is true for most of the remaining 255 experiments. In principle, similar classifications can be given when there are three or more potential causes, or when there are more than one kind of effect on each trial, or when there are trials in which both A and B are absent, but the number of distinct graphs grows superexponentially with the number of Q parameters, and no general counting principle is known for the number of Markov equivalence classes of directed acyclic graphs as a function of the number of vertices. If there are more than three trials and the Q values are constant, the same form of graphical representation can be used. If, for example, on a forth trial the experimental condition were A_4, B_4, a directed edge would be added from Q_{AB} to E_4. Further, the independence and conditional-independence relations among the Q values may imply constraints among the E variables that are not themselves independence or conditional-independence relations. Algorithms are known for identifying such constraints (Geiger, Heckerman, and Meek 1996), but they are superexponentional and infeasible for more than four variables.

9.6 Backward Blocking in the Cheng Model and Inference from Frequencies

The preceding sections give an essentially Bayesian analysis of inference in the kinds of experiments we have considered. But the basic ideas of a model of causal judgement may sometimes be paired with other methods of inference, for example, with inferences based more directly on frequencies, and the calculations involved may be quite simple.

Consider a non-Bayesian treatment of backward blocking in the context of the Cheng model. The principle I will use is this: *estimate as much as you can about the unknown quantities, or their Boolean combinations, from the data, assuming that the observed frequencies of E on various combinations of the presence or absence of the cues A and B equal the corresponding conditional probabilities of E, and assuming the Cheng model.* The principle is an uncomplicated version of an inference strategy described in Glymour (1980), there called "bootstrapping" (not to be confused with a statistical procedure of the same name) because the hypothesis to be tested is used in calculating quantities that occur in the hypothesis. Similar inferences are made every day in scientific work, and, indeed, Newton's argument for universal gravitation uses analogous methods.

Suppose that subjects are given data about the frequency of E in trials in which A and B are absent, but that there are unobserved causes U of the variation in E. They can estimate (3):

(3) $\mathrm{pr}(q_{ue} = 1) \cdot \mathrm{pr}(U) = \mathrm{fr}(E \,|\, {\sim}A, {\sim}B)$

Now suppose that they are given data about the frequency of E in the presence of both A and B. They can estimate (4):

(4) $\mathrm{pr}(q_{ae} = 1 \text{ or } q_{be} = 1)$
$$= [\mathrm{fr}(E \,|\, A, B) - \mathrm{fr}(E \,|\, {\sim}A, {\sim}B)]/(1 - \mathrm{fr}(E \,|\, {\sim}A, {\sim}B))$$

But they cannot estimate $\mathrm{pr}(q_{ae} = 1)$ or $\mathrm{pr}(q_{be} = 1)$, other than noting that these probabilities are each between 0 and $\mathrm{pr}(q_{ae} = 1 \text{ or } q_{be} = 1)$.

Suppose, finally, that they are given data about the frequency of E in the presence of A without B. Then they can estimate (5):

(5) $\mathrm{pr}(q_{ae} = 1) = [\mathrm{fr}(E \,|\, A, {\sim}B) - \mathrm{fr}(E \,|\, {\sim}A, {\sim}B)]/(1 - \mathrm{fr}(E \,|\, {\sim}A, {\sim}B))$

Further, although B was not present in the previous data, they can now also estimate $\mathrm{pr}(q_{be} = 1)$.

(6) $\mathrm{pr}(q_{be} = 1)$
$$= [\mathrm{pr}(q_{ae} = 1 \text{ or } q_{be} = 1) - \mathrm{pr}(q_{ae} = 1)]/(1 - \mathrm{pr}(q_{ae} = 1))$$
$$= [\mathrm{fr}(E \,|\, AB) - \mathrm{fr}(E \,|\, A, {\sim}B)]/[1 - \mathrm{fr}(E \,|\, A, {\sim}B)]$$

Other things equal, the closer the frequency of E when A alone is present is to the frequency of E when A and B are both present, the smaller is the estimated value of $\mathrm{pr}(q_{be} = 1)$, the causal power of B.

Note that in the case in which E always occurs if either A or B occur, the causal power of B cannot be estimated this way, because the denominator in (6) is zero. (So this method of inference would not yield backward blocking in the three-trial experiment considered previously in sections 9.3 and 9.4 of this chapter.) We have a form of backward blocking for noisy OR gates estimated with elementary algebra using Cheng's procedures, presumably not used consciously.[1]

III

Inference and Explanation in Cognitive Neuropsychology

10

Cognitive Parts: From Freud to Farah

10.1   Parts, Beliefs, and Habits: Classical Neuropsychology

Things often go wrong. People often make mistakes because they have
the wrong beliefs or desires, and when they do, the fix is symbolic, to
give them better beliefs and desires by providing information. People
often make mistakes because they have, not the wrong beliefs, but the
wrong habits or dispositions, and when they do, the fix is to train them
to form new habits. And sometimes when people and physical objects
fail to perform normally, the fix is to locate a broken or depleted part or
parts, and repair or replace them.

In the late nineteenth century there were no examples of machines that
were fixed symbolically or by training, but there were plenty of examples
of machines that worked because of the cooperation of parts, and broke
down because parts failed. And, of course, there were human models of
broken parts. The very idea of a part is of an object continuously located
in space, with special causal roles. In the paradigm cases, a part has
inputs from the external world or from other parts, inputs that change
the state of the part, and in return the part produces responses that
change the state of other parts or of the external world. There were and
are side conditions of what counts as a part, and cases that are vague or
uncertain. Stuff that tends to get used up in the operation of the machine
more rapidly than anything else does not count as a part. So the coal is
not a part of the steam engine, nor is the water or the air. Stuff that is
essential for functioning and longer lasting than fuel but shorter lasting
than wood or metal is not clearly a part, especially if it has no unam-
biguous inputs or outputs. So lubricants do not count as parts. Throttles,
wheels, axles, combustion chambers, and so on all count as parts because
they have a locale, a function, and a semipermanence.[1]

The idea that humans have parts was standard in nineteenth-century physiology—lungs, nerves, hearts, even, ambiguously, blood were thought of as parts from Harvey and even before. The great innovation of the nineteenth century was to apply the conception of parts to thought, to cognition; to suppose that the organ of thought, the brain, has cognitive parts. (The great innovation of the twentieth century was to repay the compliment by applying the idea of symbolic instruction and training to machines.). That idea was almost inevitable once materialist physiology became a going concern. For scientific legitimacy, the idea of cognitive parts required evidence of locale, evidence that a particular region or regions of the brain housed a particular part. That evidence was provided by two routes in the nineteenth century. One route was direct intervention on brains of living animals, including surgical removal of parts of the cortex and, more successfully, electrical stimulation of cortical regions. The other route, taken by Paul Broca and later by Carl Wernicke and many others, relied on nature's interventions in humans. (Broca and Wernicke respectively identified two regions of the cortex associated with two different forms of aphasia.)

The work of Broca and Wernicke inaugurated classical cognitive neuropsychology, and a number of workers—Meynert, Lissauer, Lichtheim —continued with similar investigations. Theodor Meynert, Wernicke's teacher and mentor at the University of Vienna, concluded that there must be "conduction aphasias" produced by destruction of fiber tracts connecting Broca's and Wernicke's areas. Meynert's reasoning is revealing. Damage to Wernicke's area, in the temporal lobe just posterior to the auditory cortex, was associated with inability to understand speech, although perfectly grammatical speech (often semantically jumbled) could be produced. Damage to Broca's area, in the inferior frontal gyrus, was associated with an inability to produce speech, although sounds could be perfectly well produced and speech was understood. In Wernicke's and Meynert's view, these areas did not merely house cognitive parts necessary for the respective normal functions. Rather, the cognitive parts are stations in an information-processing system. Sound is received in the auditory cortex, and its meaning is extracted in Wernicke's area. In reverse, thoughts are transformed into sentences in Broca's area. The connection between the two areas might be through other areas in the cortex responsible for the formation of thoughts, or directly through subcortical fiber tracts connecting the two areas. The latter idea led to Meynert's proposal that there should occur a distinctive aphasia—he called it "conduction aphasia"—characterized by the ability to understand, the ability to spontaneously speak, and the inability to promptly repeat meaningful speech, associated with the destruction of nerve fibers connecting Wernicke's and Broca's areas.

Wernicke's and Meynert's ideas remain one standard in neuropsychology: the brain is an information-processing system; the system is composed of localized cognitive parts; the cognitive parts function to transform some definite information—extracting meaning from sound, transforming thoughts into natural-language syntactic strings, and so on. The processes can operate in parallel and in series—you can repeat what you hear through the direct connection between Wernicke's and Broca's areas or through a slower process that goes through the association cortex. With information about the locations of cognitive parts with specific cognitive functions, brain anatomy suggests hypotheses about connections and possible dissociations, but the fundamental evidence is from the patterns of dissociations presented by clinical patients. Modern imaging technology has only modified this framework by allowing the equivalent of living autopsies.

10.2   The Connectionist Alternative

The framework developed by Wernicke and Meynert had opponents, who drew their inspiration from two sources: Cajal's revelations of the axon-dendrite structure of nerve connections and Hughlings Jackson's rather vague, holistic conception of how the brain works. The most articulate and forceful critic was Meynert's own student, Sigmund Freud. Just as the essentials of Meynert's framework remain today, the essentials of Freud's connectionist alternative in neuropsychology remain today, amplified by the ability to produce computer simulations of brain connections responsible for normal behavior, to simulate lesioning parts of the simulated brain connections, and to observe the simulated abnormalities that result. By 1895 Freud had worked out a detailed connectionist model of how the brain produces cognition, borrowing heavily from a book published in the previous year by his former colleague Sigmund Exner. Freud's model contains many (arguably most) of the central ideas of late-twentieth-century connectionist models, including a prototype of the Hebb synapse, the idea of neural Darwinism, local weight adjustment, and more. Freud's earlier published work is more directly relevant to neuropsychology and, again, is closely paralleled in arguments that appeared a century later.

In 1891 Sigmund Freud published a book-length essay entitled *On Aphasia*. In 1990 Martha Farah published a somewhat longer book-length essay, *Visual Agnosia*. A century apart, the two works are about distinct phenomena in cognitive neuropsychology, anomalies of speech, and anomalies of vision, but the books are surprisingly alike. Except for the much wider range of cases and alternative modular theories she considers, Farah's book could well have been written in 1891. Both argue for a connectionist model of mental processing, although Freud's is more radical than Farah's. They use analogous data—the cognitive deficits of nature's wretched experiments, studied individually or collectively. And they argue in similar ways. The similarities are less an indication of lack of progress in the subject than an indication of an invariance of method natural to the goals and the data.

Freud offered a connectionist critique of modular classifications and theories of speech deficits then advocated by Meynert, Wernicke, Lichtheim, and others. In 1890 Lissauer had published a modular classification and theory of visual deficits, but Freud did not discuss his work and treated only one of the phenomena—optical aphasia—discussed by Lissauer. The similarities in the strategies of argument Freud and Farah use—strategies that can be found in any number of neuropsychological publications in the last thirty five years—suggest, at least to me, that the problems and the data are naturally arranged so that certain modes of representation and argument are inevitable.

10.3   Freud

Wernicke distinguished "sensory aphasia" (Wernicke's aphasia) from "motor aphasia" (Broca's aphasia) and "conduction aphasia," supposedly associated with the destruction of nerve tracts connecting the two areas responsible for normal speech understanding and normal speech production. As elaborated by Lichtheim, the theory asserts that speech is organized according to the following diagram:

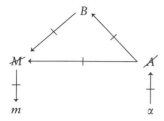

Here *a* represents the acoustic nerve. *A* represents a center responsible for the recognition of sounds. In Freud's account of Wernicke and Lichtheim, *A* stores some record of sounds, and recognition is by some unspecified mechanism of matching. *B* represents all higher-order processes that may use or produce language. *M* is the center responsible for turning thought into speech; again, according to Freud on Lichtheim, it does so by having some record of the muscular movements requisite for each sound. And *m* consists of the actual motions that produce speech. The seven slashes indicate possible lesions, each of which produces a different characteristic form of aphasia.

The short version of Freud's objection to the theory is this: (1) it implies that there are combinations of deficits that (in 1891) have not been observed, (2) it does not explain deficits that have been observed, (3) by combining lesions, almost any combination of deficits could be explained, and (4) the clinical classification of deficits is uncertain. If these objections seem to contradict one another, one should not consider the source, but rather recognize that scientists, like lawyers, often argue in the alternative. Similar complaints were made in many contexts by many authors against many theories. The methodological issues that arise when one examines the details of Freud's objections are more interesting.

Freud reports a more elaborate diagram, also due to Lichtheim:

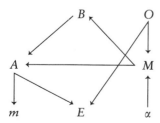

Here O represent a "centre for visual impressions." E is "the centre of cheiro-kinaesthetic impressions," whatever they are. O and its connections are responsible for the capacity for reading and for reading aloud. Freud's objection to this hypothesis is interesting and typical of Freud (later he laid a similar objection against his own theory of hysteria): "Lichtheim already knew of a common instance which he was unable to fit into his schema, i.e., the combination of motor aphasia and alexia which is too frequent to be attributed to the coincidental interruptions of two fibre tracts" (1891, 9). The remark is interesting because it at least suggests the use of frequency constraints as tests of cognitive models, but of course Freud made, and could make, no case about how frequent the combination of deficits should be.

Freud objects that while the initial diagram predicts "conduction aphasias," in which the subject can understand speech and can produce spontaneous speech but cannot repeat what he has just heard, no such cases are known: "The faculty of repeating is never lost as long as speaking and understanding are intact" (1891, 11). Instead, Wernicke's "conduction aphasias" in fact produce only paraphasia, the mistaken use of words. Freud quotes research—confirmed in modern studies— that such errors can be caused by lesions in a great many regions of the cortex, and most cases of aphasia involve paraphasia as well.

The method of argument—a certain phenomenon, whose possibility the theory requires, has not been observed—contrasts sharply with the procedure recommended by Karl Popper, the only philosopher of science who seems actually to have influenced scientists' conceptions of methodology (Peter Medawar's, for example). Popper says scientific hypotheses should be refutable by observations, but here we have a prediction that no finite set of observations can logically refute, but its failure to be verified is counted against the theory.

Freud considers, on Wernicke's and Lichtheim's behalf, another explanation of the absence of cases in which understanding and production are intact but repetition is impossible: perhaps repetition occurs through the route $M \leftarrow B \leftarrow A$ even when the route $M \leftarrow A$ is disrupted. Freud argues in the alternative that, either way, Wernicke's model does not save the phenomena. If repetition occurs through the $M \leftarrow B \leftarrow A$ route when the $M \leftarrow A$ route is disrupted, then, on the understanding of the functions of the modules, repetition of meaningful words should be retained, but the capacity to repeat nonsense should be lost. Freud says no such cases have been found, although they have been sought for. But if, in the alternative, the destruction of the $M \leftarrow A$ route breaks all connection between the two centers, then we are back to a case already unsolved.

The structure of Freud's argument introduces issues about how diagrams, or functional models, are to be interpreted. His argument depends on a particular processing role assigned to the cognitive parts, a role that makes them necessary for some activities but unnecessary for other closely related activities. And his argument introduces an issue about the gating of the human information-processing system that Wernicke and Meynert and Lichtheim propose: for normal functioning, must every pathway from input to output be intact, or just one pathway, or do different capacities have different requirements, or something else? Which inferences from what data about deficits are robust, independent of which interpretation is assumed, and which ones are not?

"Transcortical motor aphasia" is marked by inability of spontaneous speech, but repetition and reading aloud, though without understanding, are unimpaired. On Lichtheim's model, this is explained by the interruption of the $B \rightarrow M$ pathway. Against this account, Freud has an argument that, for the first time, involves an interplay between physical localization and functional localization. Freud cites a patient whose cortical damage does not accord with Lichtheim's diagram. Freud's concludes that there is no such thing as the separate centers B and A.

The argument illustrates one possible use of information about anatomical pathology, a use that goes back to Broca himself: if pieces of a diagrammatic model are identified with particular anatomical structures, then physical evidence of tissue destruction in those areas should co-occur with the corresponding deficits. In an adequate theory that modularizes function *and* localizes the functional component modules, one should be able to predict deficits from lesions and lesions from deficits. One may, of course, have perfectly consistent theories that modularize functions without localizing some (or any) of the modular components, but these cannot be theories of cognitive parts—parts do not have to be very local in a machine, they do not have to be in the same relative place in every machine that has such a part, but in each machine, they must be *somewhere*.

Freud insists at length that Lichtheim's diagram does not account for "paraphasias" (an erroneous word use). Wernicke allowed as much and suggested that these phenomena are due to a degradation but not destruction of connections. This explanation, which Freud rejects, implicitly invokes the idea that some capacities may be more fragile than other capacities that make use of the same modules, so that damage to a module may produce one incapacity but not the other. The idea seems to have been a commonplace among cognitive neuropsychologists of the day; Freud himself cites Bastian as a source. The same idea has been reborn in contemporary neuropsychology in Farah's model of optical aphasia and in Tim Shallice's proposal that some capacities require more resources of their modules than do others. The proposal, which is plausible enough in substance, raises questions about how the notion of fragility or varying resource demands can be used to make reliable inferences about mental architecture. For example, how can the differing resource requirements be determined empirically, and if they cannot, are models that postulate varying resource requirements radically underdetermined by any behavioral data?

Freud considers an intricate case of "amnesic aphasia," now called "optic aphasia"—subjects recognize objects but cannot name them. (Actually, as described, the patient also showed other agnosic deficits, for example, "he was unable to synthesize, and to perceive as wholes, object images, sound images, impressions of touch and symbols" (1891, 36). In Freud's explanation of the case, there are no centers of the kind the diagram makers proposed. Instead, there are parts of the brain that receive input from the special senses, whether vision or sound or touch, and the whole of the remainder of the cortex produces cognition by a network of connections with these input centers. Tissue destruction closer to one input source in the cortex than another—closer to the auditory input region than to the visual, say—is likelier to produce deficits in the corresponding set of capacities. But, and here is the modern part, the network does not degrade uniformly with respect to the normal cognitive capacities: some may fail from lesions while others, that work through the same network, survive. Freud thinks of perception as providing atomistic inputs that are then assembled through associations in the web. The deficits he considers are, in his terms, failures of association, not of perception. Farah, as we will see, argues that many of the agnosias are failures of perception, but the difference is largely terminological—she regards the building up of perceptual wholes from pieces as part of "perception," while Freud counts it as part of "association," but as we will also see, she thinks the *aufbau* is exactly what Freud calls "association."

There is in Freud's book a great deal more clinical detail and discussion of models of other phenomena, alexia for example, but the mode of argument and the theory are the same, and so I turn to Farah.

10.4   Farah

Farah's aim is to revise the classification of agnosics on the basis of patterns of incapacities, and from these distinctions to draw modest theoretical conclusions. Her explanation is that the agnosias chiefly result from disturbances of mid-level visual processing that normally uses either or both of two separate capacities: one for grouping spatially distributed, complex objects into wholes and another for grouping complex features of a single object. Because the data indicate a localization of pathologies and because explanations of the patterns of deficits seem to require it, her more detailed models have cognitive parts, but the parts themselves are typically association networks. Her discussion of optical aphasia may serve to illustrate the similarity of her approach to Freud's and a number of issues about representation and inference.

Optical aphasia is marked by the inability to name visually presented objects, although their function and facts about them can be correctly indicated by gesture and their written name correctly recognized and understood. Optical aphasics are able to sort visually dissimilar objects into superordinate categories and match visually presented objects by function. The ability to recognize and name objects through other modalities—sound or touch, for example—remains intact. Farah considers five different explanations of the phenomena.

The first is Ratcliff and Newcombe's model:

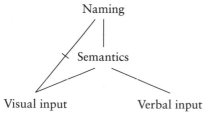

This diagram, like all of those Farah gives, is explicitly undirected but implicitly directional—the lines could properly be replaced by arrows going from lower modules to higher modules. Farah has two objections, of which I will consider only the first: no case is known in which subjects can correctly name visually presented objects but have no knowledge of the objects (1990, 135). Her objection underscores the ambiguity of the representation: Does the model presuppose that lesioning *any* pathway between visual input and naming incapacitates the ability to name from sight? If so, then the model implies that a case of the kind required in her objection is impossible, which would make her objection moot. Alternatively, does the model presuppose that only lesioning all pathways from input to output incapacitates? On that reading, the model with the single lesion does not explain optical aphasia: another lesion is required between Semantics and Naming.

A second model based on ideas of Beauvois is diagrammed this way:

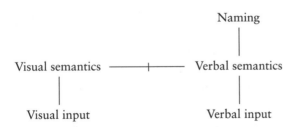

Her objection is not empirical but methodological: "The notion that we have multiple 'copies' of our entire stock of semantic knowledge, one for each modality of stimulus presentation, seems quite ad hoc, not to mention unparsimonious" (1990, 137).

A third model is taken from Riddoch and Humpreys:

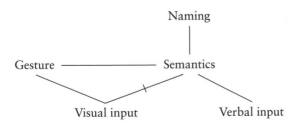

Farah has two objections: First, the model implies that optic aphasics should do poorly on categorization tasks with visually presented materials, but they do not, although it turns out that the correct empirical assessments are in some dispute. Second, the model implies that optical aphasics should not be able to make semantically correct gestures from visual presentations, but they can. Here the implicit directionality—from semantics to gesture—is essential. And another ambiguity of representation emerges. "Gesture" actually stands for two distinct kinds of performances using the same motor capacities: one performance responsive simply to the physical appearance of the visual stimulus, the other responsive to other knowledge about the object. The direct route from visual input to gesture is manifested, for example, by indicating the size of the object with one's hands and arms; the route through semantics is what is required for Charades.

A fourth model is from Coslett and Saffran:

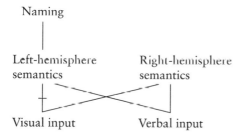

Farah makes no objection at all to this model, which differs both in connections and in the interpretation of the semantic modules from the otherwise similar model attributed to Beauvois.

The fifth model, which Farah seems to favor, is given in the following diagram:

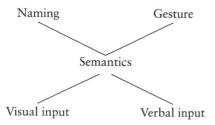

In this model, visual input, semantics, and naming are each neural networks, with their outputs connected as shown. No lesions are specified. Farah's discussion bears quoting:

The probability of success in visual naming is not simply the product of the probabilities of success in nonverbal tests of vision and nonvisual tests of naming. Vision and naming per se seem near-normal in these patients, and yet visual naming is grossly impaired. Therefore, in order to explain optic aphasia by damage at two separate loci, one must assume that effects of the damage are superadditive.

Is it completely ad hoc to suppose that the effects of damage at two separate loci would be superadditive?... The massively parallel constraint satisfaction architectures in section 5.1.3 have the ability to complete or recover partially damaged or degraded input representations, provided the damage is not too great....

It is conceivable that when a task involves activating just one damaged part of the system, the noisy output of that part can be restored, or "cleaned up" by the remaining intact network, but that when two damaged parts of the system must operate together, with the noisy output from one damaged subsystem being the input to another damaged subsystem, the recovery capabilities of the network will be exceeded and performance will drop precipitously.... Of course it must be tested empirically by building and damaging such a system, a project currently underway. (1990, 140–141)

Since it may make a difference whether a network is damaged or whether the damage is confined to the output of a network that is input to another network, the description is ambiguous among possibilities: a visual-input network whose output nodes and connections are damaged and a semantics network whose output nodes and connections are damaged (figure 10.1), or damage to the output nodes and connections of visual input and to the interior of the semantics neural net itself (figure 10.2), or damage to both network modules (figure 10.3).

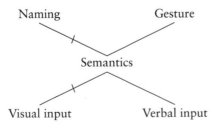

Figure 10.1

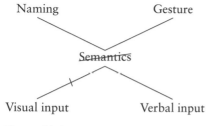

Figure 10.2

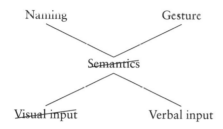

Figure 10.3

Farah's model employs a limited notion of computational resources required by a capacity. Her account does not require that some capacities demand more computational resources than others, but it does require that resources can be quantitatively degraded and that intact capacities require a minimal threshold of resources. It is a small step from there to the idea that different capacities may have different thresholds.

There is much more of methodological interest in Farah's book, but her most trenchant attack on the Wernicke/Meynert framework is in a subsequent article. There Farah formulates the hypothesis to which she objects:

The locality assumption Cognitive neuropsychologists generally assume that damage to one component of the functional architecture will have exclusively "local" effects. In other words, the undamaged components will continue to function normally, and the patient's behavior will therefore manifest the underlying impairment in a relatively direct and straightforward way. This assumption follows from a view of the cognitive architecture as being "modular" in the sense of being "informationally encapsulated" (Fodor, 1983)

... The locality assumption licenses quite direct inferences from the manifest behavioral deficit to the identity of the underlying damaged cognitive component, of the form "selective deficit in ability *A* implies component of the functional architecture dedicated to *A*." Obviously, such inferences can go awry if the selectivity of the deficit is not real, for example if the tasks testing *A* are merely harder than the comparison tasks, if there are other abilities that are not tested but which are also impaired, or if a combination of functional lesions is mistaken for a single lesion (see Shallice, 1988, ch. 10, for a thorough discussion of other possibilities for misinterpretation of dissociations within a weakly modular theoretical framework). In addition, even simple tasks tap several components at once, and properly designed control tasks are needed in order to pinpoint the deficient component, and absolve intact components downstream. However, assuming the relevant ability has been experimentally isolated, and the deficit is truly selective, the locality assumption allows us to delineate and characterize the components of the functional architecture in a direct, almost algorithmic way. (1994, 46)

In my terms, Farah's locality assumption combines three separate ideas. One is the idea of cognitive parts—discrete, causally connected, spatially localized systems whose joint normal activity creates cognitive competence. Another is the idea that the function of each cognitive part is to do a distinct piece of cognitive processing in an information processing system. The third is that the occurrence of a specific, isolated cognitive deficit indicates damage to a specific cognitive part whose function is to perform the task missing in the abnormal performance.

The last idea is gratuitous and indefensible, and Farah is right to reject it. Because an automotive part heats up abnormally, it doesn't follow that some other part whose function is to cool the abnormally hot part has failed. The inference works for the container on refrigerator trucks but not for the brakes on a wheel of your car. Her objections to the other two parts of the "locality" idea are less convincing. She analyzes three cases, and for each she offers an alternative connectionist explanation. But connectionist models can have cognitive parts, and hers do. Connectionist networks can often be resolved into topological partitions, where a topological partition divides the nodes into sets, with the members of some sets not directly connected to any of the members of certain other sets and (often, but not always) the nodes within one set all connected to one another. Farah's alternative explanations of deficit patterns all have cognitive parts of this kind, as do other attempts to give distributed representations of functional modularity. Moreover, the cognitive parts in Farah's connectionist models have distinctive cognitive functions, and she so describes them; what makes her story different from those to which she objects is that the internal mechanism of the cognitive parts she postulates is connectionist, and the cognitive functions of the parts are not directly to produce the feature absent in the deficit but, typically, to produce some other feature that, in turn and in context, normally causes the feature in deficit. Thus to explain recognition and knowledge deficits specific to living things, she postulates a cognitive part consisting of a set of nodes dedicated to "semantic knowledge of functions" and another dedicated to "visual semantic knowledge," and she postulates damage to the later, assuming that knowledge about objects involves their functions more than does knowledge about animals.

Farah's contrast between "parallel distributed processing" and "locality" is partly spurious in substance but substantive in methodology. In practice, both rely on cognitive parts and differ only in the details (and amount of detail) of the models. There are, however, real alternatives. One of them is Freud's, which almost no one now endorses, in which the cortex is a single connectionist structure with no discernible substructures with distinct functions. Another is one Farah seems to take seriously: "Finally, even if PDP were false, there remain other ways of conceptualizing human information processing that provide explicit, mechanistic alternatives to modularity. For example, in production system architectures (see Klahr, Langley & Neches, 1987) working memory is highly nonencapsulated" (1994, 59).

Production system "architectures" for cognition do not have cognitive parts, because there is no implied organic locality for their data structures. A program written for your computer in Pascal or LISP or whatever may involve a lot of data structures, but their implementation is scattered over the memory chips of your machine, and has no finer locale. The same is true with ACT* and SOAR, because these "theories" are simply programming languages with some built-in, automated processing. They cannot and do not account for patterns of neuropsychological deficits.

10.5   Issues

The diagrams that neuropsychologists have used for more than a century to represent the hypothetical causal relations among hypothetical cognitive parts are causal Bayes nets. The values of the variables are often unclearly specified, but they can usually be reconstructed as 2-valued, one value for normal input or output and another for abnormal input or output. The hypothesis that the brain produces cognitive competence through the action of cognitive parts is the indispensable minimum in cognitive neuropsychology—even if the parts themselves are neural nets —and that is why, whether recognized or denied, the assumption and the diagrams are ubiquitous.

Brain anatomy and the character of deficits may suggest various diagrams and hypotheses about the functions of their hypothetical parts, but the fundamental methodological question is whether, and how, patterns of deficits can distinguish among alternative diagrams. The questions have been bitterly debated in the neuropsychological literature, usually by citing slogans from the philosophy of science or by debating particular examples. As the neuropsychologists have framed them, the questions can be divided into two sorts: what can surveys of patterns of deficits exhibited by individuals tell us about "cognitive architecture," and what can comparisons of measures for different groups of people tell us. To these questions I will add a third. Reversing Freud's complaint against Lichtheim, it is often complained that neural net models can "explain anything." Can lesioning causal Bayes nets "explain anything," or are there natural explanatory limitations? The next three chapters examine these questions from fresh viewpoints, emphasizing, for the first two issues, the central point: how to get to the truth, whatever it may be.

11

Inferences to Cognitive Architecture from Individual Case Studies

11.1 The Issues

Neuropsychology has relied on a variety of methods to obtain information about human "cognitive architecture" from the profiles of capacities and incapacities presented by normal and abnormal subjects. The nineteenth-century neuropsychological tradition associated with Broca, Wernicke, Meynert, and Lichtheim attempted to correlate abnormal behavior with loci of brain damage, and thus to found syndrome classification ultimately on neuroanatomy. At the same time, they aimed to use the data of abnormal cognitive incapacities to found inferences to the functional architecture of the normal human cognitive system. Contemporary work in neuropsychology involves statistical studies of the correlation of behavior with physical measures of brain activity in both normal and abnormal subjects, statistical studies of the correlations of behavioral abnormalities in groups of subjects, and studies of behavioral abnormalities in particular individuals, sometimes in conjunction with information about the locations of lesions.[1] The goal of identifying the functional structure of normal cognitive architecture remains as it was in the nineteenth century.

The fundamental methodological issues about the enterprise of cognitive neuropsychology concern the characterization of methods by which features of normal cognitive architecture can be identified from any of the kinds of data just mentioned, the assumptions upon which the reliability of such methods are premised, and the limits of such methods—even granting their assumptions—in resolving uncertainties about that architecture. These questions have recently been the subject of intense debate occasioned by a series of articles by Caramazza and his collaborators (1984, 1986, 1988, 1989); these articles have prompted a number of responses, including at least one book. As the issues have been framed in these exchanges, they concern the following:

• Whether studies of the statistical distribution of abnormalities in groups of subjects selected by syndrome, by the character of brain lesions, or by other means, are relevant evidence for determining cognitive architecture
• Whether the proper form of argument in cognitive neuropsychology is "hypothetico-deductive"—in which a theory is tested by deducing from it consequences whose truth or falsity can be determined more or less directly—or "bootstrap testing"—in which theories are tested by assuming parts of them and using those parts to deduce (noncircularly) from the data instances of other parts of the theory
• Whether associations of capacities, or cases of dissociation in which one of two normally concurrent capacities is absent, or double dissociations in which of two normally concurrent capacities A and B, one abnormal subject possesses capacity A but not B, while another abnormal subject possesses B but not A, are the "more important" form of evidence about normal cognitive architecture

Bub and Bub (1991) object that Caramazza's arguments against group studies assume a "hypothetico-deductive" picture of theory testing in which a hypothesis is confirmed by a body of data if from the hypothesis (and perhaps auxiliary assumptions) a description of the data can be deduced. They suggest that inference to cognitive architecture from neuropsychological data follows instead a "bootstrap" pattern much like that described by Glymour (1980). They, and also Shallice (1988), reassert that double-dissociation data provide especially important evidence for cognitive architecture. Shallice argues that if a functional module underlying two capacities is a connectionist computational system where one capacity requires more computational resources than another, then injuries to the module that remove one of these capacities may leave the other intact. The occurrence of subjects having one of these capacities and lacking the other (dissociation) will therefore not permit a decision as to whether or not there is a functional module required for the first capacity but not required for the second. Double dissociations, Shallice claims, do permit this decision.

The main issue in these disputes is this: by what methods, and from what sorts of data, can the truth about various questions of cognitive architecture be found, whatever the truth may be? There is a tradition in computer science and in mathematical psychology that provides a means for resolving such questions. Work in this tradition characterizes mathematically whether or not specific questions can be settled in principle from specific kinds of evidence. Positive results are proved by exhibiting some method and demonstrating that it can reliably reach the truth; negative results are proved by showing that no possible method can do so. There are results of these kinds about the impossibility of predicting the behavior of a "black box" with an unknown Turing machine inside, about the possibility of such predictions when the black box is known to contain a finite automaton rather than a Turing machine, about the indistinguishability of parallel and serial procedures for short-term memory phenomena, about which classes of mathematically possible languages could and could not be learned by humans, about whether a computationally bounded system can be distinguished from an uncomputable system by any behavioral evidence about the logical limits of the propositions that can be resolved by any learner, and much more (see Kelly 1996 for a review and references to the literature). However abstract and remote from practice such results may seem, they address the logical essence of questions about discovery and relevant evidence. From this point of view, disputes in cognitive neuropsychology about one or another specific form of argument are well motivated but ill directed: they are focused on the wrong questions.

From what sorts of evidence, and with what sorts of background assumptions, can questions of interest in cognitive psychology be resolved, no matter what the answer to them may be, by some possible method, and from what sorts of evidence and background assumptions can they not be resolved by any possible method? With some idealization, the question of the capacities of various experimental designs in cognitive neuropsychology to uncover cognitive architecture can be reduced to comparatively simple questions about the prior assumptions investigators are willing to make. The point of this chapter is to present some of the simplest of those reductions.

11.2   Theories as Functional Diagrams and Graphs

Neuropsychological theories typically assume that the brain instantiates "functional modules" that have specific roles in producing cognitive

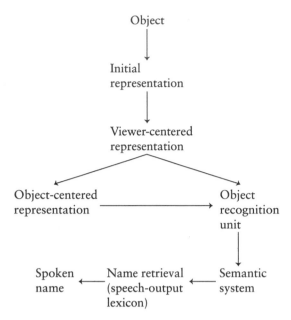

Figure 11.1
Functional model for object recognition

behavior. In the processes that produce cognitive behavior, some of the output of some modules is sent as input to other modules until eventually the task behavior is produced. Various hypothetical functional modules have standard names, e.g., the "phonemic buffer," and come with accounts of what they are thought to do. Such theories or "models" are often presented by diagrams. For example, Ellis and Young (1988) consider the "functional model" for object recognition given in figure 11.1.

In explaining profiles of normal capacities and abnormal incapacities with the aid of such a diagram, the modules and their connections are understood to be embedded in a larger structure that serves as a kind of *deus ex machina* in producing particular inputs or particular outputs. For example, a subject's capacity to name familiar objects in experimental trials is explained by assuming that presentation of the object is supplied as input to this diagram, and that the subject has somehow correctly processed the instruction "Name the object before you," and that this processing has adjusted the parameters of the functional modules and their connections so that the subject will indeed attempt to name the object. None of the instructional processing is represented in the diagram. Further, it is understood that the modules represented in such diagrams are connected to other possible outputs that are not represented, and that with different instructional processing, the very same stimulus would activate a different collection of paths that would result in a different output. For example, if the subject were instructed "Copy the object before you" and processed this information normally, then the presentation of the object would bring about an attempt to draw the object rather than to speak its name.

In effect, most parts of theories of cognitive architecture are tacit, and the normal behavior to be expected from a set of instructions and a stimulus can only be inferred from the descriptions given of the internal modules. For example, when Ellis and Young describe an internal module as the "speech-output lexicon," we assume that it must be activated in any process producing coherent speech, but not in processes producing coherent writing or in the processes of understanding speech, writing, or gestures. Evidently, it is a great convenience and a practical necessity to leave much of the theory tacit and indicated only by descriptions of internal modules, although the descriptions may sometimes occasion misunderstanding, equivocation, and unprofitable disputes.

The practice of cognitive neuroscience makes a considerable use of scientists' capacities to exploit descriptions of hypothetical internal modules in order to contrive experiments that test a particular theory. Equally, the skills of practitioners are required to distinguish various kinds or features of stimuli as belonging properly to different inputs, which means that these features are processed differently under the same set of instructions. I propose to leave these features of the enterprise to one side and to assume for the moment that everyone agrees as to what stimulus conditions should be treated as inputs to a common input channel in the normal cognitive architecture, and that everyone agrees as to what behaviors should be treated as outputs from a common output channel.

It is also clear that in practice there are often serious ambiguities about the range of performance that constitutes normal or abnormal behavior, and that much of the important work in cognitive neuropsychology consists in resolving such ambiguities. I will also put these matters to one side and assume that all such issues are settled, and that there is agreement as to which behaviors count as abnormal in a setting, and which normal.

With these rather radical idealizations, what can investigation of the patterns of capacities and incapacities in normal and abnormal subjects tell us about the normal architecture?

11.3   Formalities

The diagram in figure 11.2 is also given by Ellis and Young (1988). The idea is that a signal, auditory or visual, enters the system, and various things are done to it; the double arrows indicate that the signal is passed back and forth, the single arrows indicate that it is passed in only one

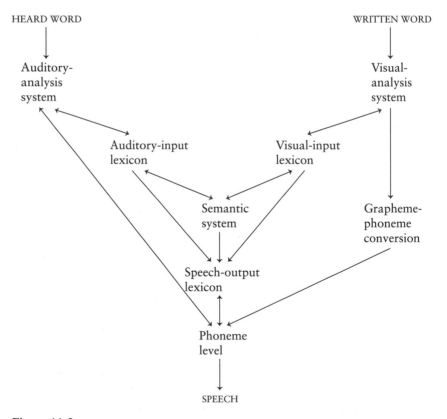

Figure 11.2

direction. If any path through the semantic system from the input channel is disrupted while the rest of the system remains intact, then the remaining paths to the phoneme level will enable the subject to repeat a spoken word or pronounce a written word, but not to understand it.

The evidence offered for a diagram consists of profiles of capacities that are found among people with brain injuries. There are people who can repeat spoken words but cannot recognize them, people who can recognize spoken words but can't understand them, people who show parallel incapacities for written words, people who can repeat or recognize or understand spoken words but not written, and people with the reverse capacities. What is the logic of inferences from profiles of this kind to graphs or diagrams? To investigate that question it will help to standardize diagrams.

Performances whose appearance or failure (under appropriate inputs) is used in evidence will be explicitly represented as vertices in the graphs, and the corresponding stimuli or inputs will be likewise distinguished. So where Ellis and Young have an output channel labeled simply "speech," I will have output nodes labeled "repeats," "repeats with recognition," "repeats with understanding." In any context that a psychologist would identify a normal capacity, I will place a corresponding set of input nodes and an output node. This convention in no way falsifies the problem, for such relations are certainly implicit in the theory that goes with the conventional diagram; I am only making things a bit more explicit. Second, I will assume for the time being that each represented pathway from input to output is *essential* for a normal capacity. There are certainly examples in the literature of capacities that have alternative pathways, either of which will produce the appropriate output. I will ignore this complication for the moment, but not forever.

The system of hypothetical modules and their connections form a *directed graph*, that is, a set V of vertices or nodes and a set E of ordered pairs of vertices, each ordered pair representing a *directed edge* from the first member of the pair to the second. Some of the vertices represent inputs that can be given to a subject in an experimental task, and some of the vertices represent measures of behavioral responses. Everything in between, which is to say most of the directed graph that represents the cognitive architecture, is unobserved. Each vertex between input and behavioral response can represent a very complicated structure that may be localized in the brain or may somehow be distributed; each directed edge represents a pathway by which information is communicated. That assumption requires replacing bidirected edges with two edges, one in each direction, but nothing is lost thereby.

Such a directed graph may be a theory of the cognitive architecture of normals; the architecture of abnormals is obtained by supposing that one or more of the vertices or directed edges of the normal graph has been removed. Any individual subject is assumed to instantiate some such graph. In the simplest case, we can think of the output nodes of as taking values 0 and 1, where the value 1 obtains when the subject exhibits the behavior expected of normal subjects for appropriate inputs and instructions, and the value of 0 obtains for abnormal behavior in those circumstances. I will call a *capacity* any pair $\langle I, O \rangle$, where O is an output variable (or vertex) and I is an input vertex, such that in normal architecture there is a directed path from I to O.

Between input and output a vast number of alternative graphs of hypothetical cognitive architecture are possible a priori. The fundamental inductive task of cognitive psychology, including cognitive neuropsychology, is to describe the intervening structure common to normal humans.

To begin with, I make some simplifying assumptions about the directed graph that represents normal human cognitive architecture. I will later consider how some of them can be altered.

Assumption 1   Assume that the behavioral response variables take only 0 or 1 as values, where the value 1 means, roughly, that the subject exhibits normal competence and the value 0 means that the subject does not exhibit normal competence.

Assumption 2   Assume that all normal subjects have the same graph, i.e., the same cognitive architecture.

Assumption 3   Assume that the graph of the cognitive architecture of any abnormal subject is a *subgraph* of the normal graph, i.e., is a graph obtained by deleting either edges or vertices (and, of course, all edges containing any deleted vertex) or both in the normal graph.

Assumption 4   The default value of all output nodes—the value they exhibit when they have not been activated by a cognitive process—is 0.

Assumption 5   If any path from a relevant input variable to an output variable that occurs in the normal graph is missing in an abnormal graph, the abnormal subject will output the value 0 for that output variable on inputs for which the normal subject outputs 1 for that variable.

Assumption 6 Every subgraph of the normal graph will eventually occur among abnormal subjects.

These assumptions are in some respects unrealistic, and in some ways less unrealistic than they might at first appear. One might object to the assumption that all pathways in a graph between input and output must be intact for the normal capacity, and substitute instead the requirement that for normal capacities at least one pathway must be intact. I will later describe what results from this alternative, or from assuming ignorance as to which of these gatings is correct. For the purpose of the analysis, it does not matter whether the pathway to a node inhibits or promotes some response, so long as when all pathways are intact, the response is counted as normal, and when one of them is removed, the response, whatever it may be, is counted as abnormal. Nor is it unrealistic to assume that inputs and outputs take values 0 and 1 only. The input node identifies a particular task condition, and 1 on the input node simply codes that the task is demanded and the relevant stimulus supplied. The subject's performance, whatever it may be, is either counted as normal, in which case the output node has value 1, or it is not, in which case the output node has value 0.

The structures that satisfy these axioms are causal Bayes nets if the graph is acyclic. The structures that result from lesioning any such acyclic diagram are causal Bayes nets with interventions. The problem of inference is to reliably determine which of a collection of alternative causal explanations of this kind is true from data generated with and without interventions, when the nature of the intervention, if any, is unobserved.

11.4 Discovery Problems and Success

We want to know when, subject to these assumptions, features of normal cognitive architecture can be identified from the profiles of the behavioral capacities and incapacities of normals and abnormals. It is useful to be a little more precise about what we wish to know, so as to avoid some likely confusions.

I will say that a *discovery problem* consists of a collection of alternative conceivable graphs of normal cognitive architecture. As far as we know a priori, any graph in the collection may be the true normal cognitive architecture. We want our methods to be able to extract as much information as possible about the true structure, or to be able to answer some question about the true structure, no matter which graph in the collection it is. Whichever graph may actually describe normal architecture, the scientist receives examples, normal subjects, who instantiate the normal graph and examples, abnormal subjects, who instantiate various subgraphs of the normal graph. For each subject, the scientist obtains a *profile* of that subject's capacities and incapacities. So, abstractly, we can think of the scientist as obtaining a sequence of capacity profiles, where the maximal profiles (those with the most capacities) are all from the true but unknown normal graph, and other profiles are from subgraphs of that normal graph.

We have assumed that eventually the scientist will see every profile of capacities associated with any subgraph of the normal graph, although nothing in our assumptions implies that the scientist will *know* when profiles of every subgraph of the normal graph have been observed. Let us suppose, as is roughly realistic, that the profiles are obtained in a sequence, with some (perhaps all) profiles being repeated. After each stage in the sequence, let the scientist (or a method) conjecture the answer to a question about the cognitive architecture. No matter how many distinct profiles have been observed at any stage of inquiry, the scientist may not be sure that further distinct profiles are impossible. We cannot be sure at any particular time (save in special cases) that circumstance has provided us with every possible combination of injuries, separating all of the capacities that could possibly be separated. Hence, if by success in discovering the normal cognitive architecture we mean that after some finite stage of inquiry the scientist will be able to specify that architecture and know that the specification will not be refuted by any further evidence, success is generally impossible. We should instead require something weaker for success: the scientist should eventually reach the right answer by a method that disposes her to stick with the right answer ever after, even though she may not know when that point has been reached.

I will say that a method of conjecturing the cognitive architecture (or conjecturing an answer to a question about that architecture) *succeeds* on a discovery problem posed by a collection of alternative hypothetical architectures if for each of these architectures, and for each possible ordering (into an unbounded sequence) of the profiles of normals and abnormals associated with that architecture, there is a point after which the method always conjectures the true architecture or always answers the question correctly. In other words, if we think of a method of inference as an infinite series of conjectures in response to an ever increasing sequence of data, the number of erroneous conjectures is finite. If no method can succeed on a discovery problem, I will say the problem is *unsolvable*.

On first encounter, this idea of success in inquiry may be confusing, and a simple example may help. Let the data consist of facts about the color of particular emeralds, given in arbitrary order. Consider the hypotheses "All emeralds are green" and "Some emerald is not green" and imagine a method of investigation that seeks to settle the question *with certainty* after seeing some finite number of emeralds. In application, the conjectures of the method can be withheld until enough data have been acquired so that the method is certain, and then the answer can be announced. By the very characterization of the method, there must be a number n of green emeralds such that if that number is seen and no emerald of any other color is seen, the method must announce with certainty that all emeralds are green. Such a method cannot be correct in all possible circumstances, consistent with our ignorance at the beginning of inquiry. For one possible circumstance is that the first n emeralds are green and the next is not, and in that circumstance the method will fail. We assumed nothing about the method except that it acts only on the data and that it produces a conjecture after some finite amount of evidence is seen, a conjecture that purports to be correct no matter what. So no such method exists.

Our little argument is the problem of induction in the form given it first by Plato and later by Sextus Empiricus. It is the reason why Karl Popper insisted that the aim of science could only be to falsify theories—which he took to make universal claims—but not to verify them. Yet in cognitive neuropsychology, many of the important hypotheses are existential—models of normal architecture imply that certain combinations of deficits should exist, and the failure to find them is used in arguments against the model. This is a kind of inference that Popper's methodology does not allow. But we can allow it if we weaken the requirement of success in inquiry from that of finding the right answer with certainty after a finite amount of evidence is seen to the requirement that our method of conjecture eventually settle upon the truth and stick with the truth ever after, even if we do not know when the truth has been reached. That is exactly what is done by the requirement of success proposed above. To solve the problem about emeralds, we can adopt the method that conjectures that all emeralds are green so long as all emeralds so far observed are green, and that says that there is an emerald of another color ever after one of that color is seen. If we occupy a world in which there is a nongreen emerald, then by assumption, it will eventually turn up in the data, and our method will give the true answer ever after. If, to the contrary, we occupy a world in which all emeralds are green, our method will forever conjecture that all emeralds are green, and it will always be right.

Probabilistic accounts of inquiry and methodology are undoubtedly more familiar. The procedure most routinely used in psychology is hypothesis testing, which, however, is not a method of inquiry: hypothesis testing tells us, at best, what hypotheses to reject, but itself provides no reliable method of finding any positive truth, either in the short run or the long run. A less familiar but more thoroughgoing probabilistic account of method is Bayesian. It would have us, before any data is seen, put a probability distribution over the hypotheses, and also specify for each hypothesis the probability of any finite sequence of data, conditional on the truth of the hypothesis. This initial, or prior, probability distribution is then changed as data is acquired, by computing the probability of each hypothesis, conditional on the evidence so far seen.

From the Bayesian perspective, reliability consists in converging toward probability 1 for the true hypothesis, no matter what the truth may be from among the alternatives considered at the outset. As it turns out, that success criterion is here equivalent to the one I have proposed: if there is a method that solves a discovery problem, in the sense defined, then there is a prior probability distribution whose conditional distributions converge to 1 for the true hypothesis on every possible data sequence. The converse is equally true: if Bayesian convergence is possible, then the discovery problem is solvable in the sense defined. What this means for theoretical (and practical) analysis is this: so long as we are concerned with finding the truth, whatever it is, in settings of the kind we are considering in this chapter, we do not have to complicate matters with probability calculations.

11.5 An Illustration

The role of these ideas in understanding the power and limits of idealized individual data in cognitive neuropsychology can be illustrated by considering a discovery problem, given by six alternative graphs, schematizing hypotheses about the normal cognitive architecture involved in four normal capacities. The graphs are given in figure 11.3. All of these graphs allow the same normal profile: $N = \{\langle I_1, O_1 \rangle, \langle I_1, O_2 \rangle, \langle I_2, O_1 \rangle, \langle I_2, O_2 \rangle\}$. With each of these graphs there is associated the subgraphs that can be formed by lesioning one or more edges or vertices, and each subgraph will have a characteristic set of deficits—interrupted normal capacities. Note the similarity to the graphs for optical aphasia in chapter 10.

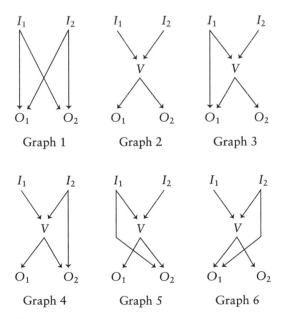

Figure 11.3

Each normal graph entails constraints on the profiles that can occur in abnormals. Graph 1, for example, entails the empty set of constraints; every subset of N is allowable as an abnormal profile if graph 1 represents the normal architecture. Graph 2 imposes strong constraints: if an abnormal has two intact capacities that together involve both inputs and both outputs, then he must have all of the normal capacities. Graph 3 allows that an abnormal may be missing $\langle I_1, O_1 \rangle$ while all other capacities are intact. Graph 4 allows that an abnormal may be missing the capacity $\langle I_2, O_2 \rangle$ while all other capacities are intact. We have the following inclusion relations among the sets of allowable (normal and abnormal profiles) associated with each graph: The set of profiles allowed by graph 1 includes those allowed by graphs 3 and 4. The set of profiles allowed by graph 4 is not included in and does not include the set of profiles allowed by graph 3. The sets of profiles allowed by graphs 3 and 4 both include the set of profiles allowed by graph 2. And so on.

To make matters as clear as possible, I give a list of the profiles that the six graphs permit, where a profile is a subset of the four capacities, and the capacities (I_i, O_j) are identified as ordered pairs i, j. The set of all possible profiles is given in table 11.1.

Table 11.1
The set of all possible profiles

Profile	Capacities			
N	1, 1	1, 2	2, 1	2, 2
P_1	1, 1	1, 2	2, 1	
P_2	1, 1	1, 2		2, 2
P_3	1, 1		2, 1	2, 2
P_4		1, 2	2, 1	2, 2
P_5	1, 1	1, 2		
P_6	1, 1		2, 1	
P_7		1, 2	2, 1	
P_8	1, 1			2, 2
P_9		1, 2		2, 2
P_{10}			2, 1	2, 2
P_{11}	1, 1			
P_{12}		1, 2		
P_{13}			2, 1	
P_{14}				2, 2
P_{15}				

Graph 1 Abnormals with every profile occur.
Graph 2 Abnormals with P_5, P_6, P_9-P_{15} occur.
Graph 3 Abnormals with P_4, P_5, P_6, and P_9-P_{15} occur.
Graph 4 Abnormals with P_1, P_5, P_6, and P_9-P_{15} occur.
Graph 5 Abnormals with P_3, P_5, P_6, and P_9-P_{15} occur.
Graph 6 Abnormals with P_2, P_5, P_6, and P_9-P_{15} occur.

The following procedure solves the discovery problem: *conjecture any normal graph whose set of normal and abnormal profiles includes all the profiles seen in the data but has no proper subset of profiles (associated with one of the graphs) that also includes all of the profiles seen in the data.*

We have seen examples from the nineteenth century through the end of the twentieth in which a normal capacity was held to be intact provided *at least one* pathway from input to output was intact. Such theories can be analyzed by replacing assumption 5 above with the assumption, call it 5*, that abnormal output occurs if and only if *all* pathways from input to output are interrupted, or more generally, with the assumption that, for each normal capacity, one of assumptions 5 and 5* holds. The last alternative is the most interesting, and amounts to having to learn both the topology and the gating. The sets of profiles that can be obtained from the six graphs by lesioning, under assumption 5*, are as follows:

Graph 1 Abnormals with every profile occur. The gatings for this structure are the same under assumption 5 or 5*.
Graph 2 Abnormals with P_5, P_6, and P_9-P_{15} occur. The gatings for this structure are the same under assumption 5 or 5*.
Graph 3 Abnormals with P_2, P_3, P_5, P_6, P_8-P_{15} occur.
Graph 4 Abnormals with P_2, P_3, P_5, P_6, P_8-P_{15} occur.
Graph 5 Abnormals with P_1, P_4, P_5, P_6, P_7, P_9-P_{15} occur.
Graph 6 Abnormals with P_1, P_4, P_5, P_6, P_7, P_9-P_{15} occur.

Under the gating of assumption 5*, in which a capacity is disabled only if all paths from input to output are interrupted, graphs 3 and 4 cannot be distinguished, and graphs 5 and 6 cannot be distinguished. The discovery problem posed by the six graphs under this gating is unsolvable. The best procedure, is to guess the indistinguishability class with the smallest set of abnormal profiles that includes all abnormal profiles so far observed.

What about the discovery problems posed by the twelve structures consisting of the six graphs each with the two alternative gatings, 5 and 5*? The task is then to determine the graph *and* the gating. Gatings 5 and 5* are the same for graphs 1 and 2. For the remaining four graphs the gatings are distinct, and which of the gatings is correct can be inferred from the observed profiles: gating 5* requires in these cases that P_7 or P_8 occur, while neither profile can occur with gating 5 for graphs 3, 4, 5, and 6. Save for the indistinguishable pairs under gating 5*, all distinct graph/gating pairs have distinct profile sets and, up to that indistinguishability, the combined problem can be solved.

11.6 Complications

There are at least three other ways in which indistinguishable structures can occur: The edges coming into a vertex V can be pinched together at a new vertex V' and a directed edge from V' to V introduced. The edges coming out of a vertex V can be moved so that they are out of a new vertex V' and an edge from V to V' introduced. And finally, a vertex V can be replaced by a subgraph G such that every edge in V is replaced by an edge into G, every edge out of V is replaced by an edge out of G, and every input to G has a path in G to every output of G. Each of these operations results in a graph that is indistinguishable from the original graph in the normal and abnormal profiles it allows. The first two operations are really only special ways of thinking about the third. For example, the following graph is indistinguishable from graph 3 under gating 5:

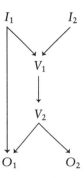

One of the ideas of cognitive neuropsychology is that one and the same module can be involved in the processing of quite different inputs related to quite different outputs. For example, a general "semantic system" may be involved in speech processing, but it may also be involved in writing or nonverbal tasks. Some of the input channels that are relevant to a nonverbal task that accesses the "semantic system" may not be input channels for a verbal task that accesses the "semantic system." Although there is in the diagram or graph a directed path from input channels particular to nonverbal tasks to the output channels of verbal tasks, those inputs are nonetheless irrelevant to the verbal task. Formally, the idea is that in addition to the directed graph structure, there is what I shall call a *relevance structure*, which determines that a given output variable depends on some of the input variables to which it is connected in the directed graph but not on other input variables to which it is so connected. The relevance structure is simply part of the theory the cognitive scientist provides. One and the same output variable can have several distinct relevant input sets. Whenever two capacities have the same output variable, we can "pinch" any subset of their paths and obtain an indistinguishable graph (figure 11.4).

Of course, the possibilities are not restricted to a single pinch. There can be any grouping of lines, and there can be hierarchies of intermediate nodes. The space of possibilities is *very* large. The number of ways of introducing extra vertices that are immediate between the inputs and a single output is an exponential function of size of that set. And, of course, directed edges between intermediate vertices at the same level can be introduced. One possible view about such indeterminacies is, of

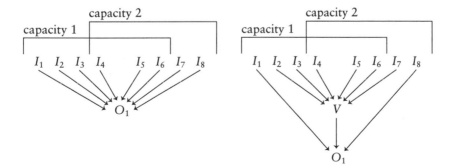

Figure 11.4

course, that they represent substructure that is unresolvable by cognitive neuropsychology. Bub and Bub (1991) have suggested that if for each internal module there is an input/output pair specific to that module, then the entire graph structure can be identified, and that seems correct if extraordinarily optimistic.

There are further generalizations that I will not pursue. Jeff Bub has suggested that any model comes with a specified set of sets of paths from input to output such that all members of at least one set must be intact in order for the corresponding capacity to be intact. Given any set of alternatives of this kind, there is a mathematical fact of the matter of whether they can be reliably distinguished from deficit patterns, but, of course, there can be no very interesting completely general theorems about discovery in such a range of cases. There is, however, no reason why learning-theoretic analyses need be confined to my simple examples. As is customary in most of the neuropsychological literature, I have assumed throughout that the relations among the cognitive parts are deterministic. A more generalized picture would allow probability distributions; in that case the purely deterministic inference methods described here might give way to probabilistic methods.

The conclusion seems to be that under the assumptions considered, a good many features of cognitive architecture can in principle be distinguished from studies of individuals and the profiles of their capacities, although a graph cannot be distinguished from an alternative that has a functionally redundant structure. Under those assumptions, several of Caramazza's claims are essentially correct: He is correct that the essential question is not whether the data are associations, dissociations, or double dissociations; the essential question is what profiles occur in the data. He is correct that from data on individuals one can solve some discovery problems. In any particular issue framed by assumptions of this kind, an explicit characterization of the alternatives held to be possible a priori and clear formulation in graph-theoretic terms of the discovery problem at issue would permit a definite decision as to whether the question can be answered in the limit, and by what procedures.

11.7   Resource/PDP Models

A picture of the brain that has a long history supposes that regions of the brain function as parallel distributed processors, and receive inputs and pass outputs to modules in other regions. Thus the vertices of the graphs of cognitive architecture that we have thus far considered would be interpreted as something like parallel-distributed-processing networks (McClelland et al. 1986). These "semi-PDP" models suggest a different connection between brain damage and behavioral incapacities than is given by our previous assumptions. A familiar fact about PDP networks is that a network trained to identify a collection of concepts may suffer differential degradation when some of its "neurons" are removed. With such damage, the network may continue to be able to make some inferences correctly but be unable to perform others. Thus a "semi-PDP" picture of mental functioning argues that damage to a vertex in a graph of cognitive architecture is damage to some of the neurons of a network and may result in the elimination of some capacities that involve that vertex, but not others. Shallice (1988), for example, has endorsed such a picture, and he uses it to argue for the special importance of double-dissociation phenomena in cognitive neuropsychology. He suggests that some capacities may be more difficult or computationally demanding than others, and hence more easily disrupted. Double dissociations, he argues, show that of two capacities, at least one of them uses some module not involved in the other capacity.

Consider whether, under this hypothesis, information about profiles of capacities and incapacities permits us to discover anything at all about cognitive architecture.

With each vertex or edge of the normal graph we should imagine a *partial ordering* of the capacities that involve that edge or vertex. That capacity 1 is *less than or equal to* capacity 2 in the partial ordering indicates that any damage to that edge or vertex that removes capacity 1 also removes capacity 2. If capacity 1 is less than or equal to capacity 2 and capacity 2 is less than or equal to capacity 1, then any injury to the module that removes one capacity will remove the other. If capacity 1 is less than or equal to capacity 2 for some edge or vertex, but capacity 2 is not less than or equal to capacity 1 for that edge or vertex, then capacity 1 is *less than* capacity 2 for that edge or vertex, meaning that capacity 2 can be removed by damage to that element without removing capacity 1. If capacity 1 is not less than or equal to capacity 2 for some edge or vertex and capacity 2 is also not less than or equal to capacity 1 for that edge or vertex, then they are *unordered* for that graph element, meaning that some injury to that graph element can remove capacity 1 without removing capacity 2, and some injury to that graph element can remove capacity 2 without removing capacity 1. A degenerate case of a partial ordering leaves all capacities unordered. I will call a graph in which there is attached to each vertex and directed edge a partial ordering (including possibly the degenerate ordering) of the capacities involving that graph element a *partially ordered graph*.

The set of objects in a discovery problem are now not simply directed graphs representing alternative possible normal cognitive architectures. The objects are instead partially ordered graphs, where one and the same graph may appear in the problem with many different orderings of capacities attached to its edges and vertices. The presence of such alternatives indicates an absence of background knowledge as to which capacities are more computationally demanding than others. I will assume that the goal of inference remains to identify the true graph structure.

Rather than forming abnormal structures by simply deleting edges or vertices, an injury is implicitly represented by *labeling* a directed edge or vertex with the set of damaged capacities involving that edge or vertex. The profile of capacities associated with such a damaged labeled graph excludes the labeled capacities. Depending on whether or not there is a partial ordering of capacities or outputs attached to graph elements, there are restrictions on the possible labelings. When there are partial orderings, a discovery problem is posed by a collection of labeled graphs.

On these assumptions alone the enterprise of identifying modular structure from patterns of deficits seems hopeless: even the simplest graph structures become indistinguishable. An easy illustration is given

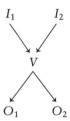

Figure 11.5
If (I_1, O_1) is more demanding (i.e., greater) than all other capacities, profile P_4 is added. If (I_1, O_2) is more demanding than all other capacities, profile P_3 is added. If (I_2, O_1) is more demanding than all other capacities, profile P_2 is added. If (I_2, O_2) is more demanding than all other capacities, profile P_1 is added.

by six graphs in figure 11.3. Consider what happens when the discovery problem under the gating of assumption 5 is expanded by adding to graph 2 some possible orderings of the computational demands placed on the internal module V by the four capacities considered in this example (see figure 11.5).

Thus, in addition to the profiles previously allowed by graph 2, any one of the four profiles characteristic of graphs 3 through 6 may appear, depending on which capacity places the greatest computational demands on the internal module. If all capacities are equally fragile, the set of profiles originally associated with graph 2 is obtained; still other profiles can be obtained if orderings of the internal module of graph 2 are combined with orderings of the directed edges in that graph. Similar things are true of graphs 3 to 6. Thus, unless one has strong prior knowledge as to which capacities are the most computationally demanding (for every module), even simple discovery problems appear hopeless.

12
Group Data in Cognitive Neuropsychology

12.1 Introduction

According to Alfonso Caramazza and a number of other neuropsychologists, statistical studies that compare the behavior of different groups of brain damaged people, or that compare brain damaged groups with normal groups, are of no value to cognitive neuropsychology and are apt to introduce erroneous conjectures. The principal trouble with group studies, the objection goes, is that a group of Broca's aphasics may be a mixture of people who have suffered different sorts of damage to their cognitive systems, and who therefore produce in different ways the configuration of deficits characteristic of the syndrome. At best, they claim, group studies throw away the valuable information about individuals, and at worst, they form the basis for utterly erroneous inferences about the organization of mind.

Disputes of this kind are not entirely new; in different forms they ran through nineteenth-century psychology, physiology, and scientific medicine. Claude Bernard ridiculed the use of statistical hypotheses in physiology, which he regarded as a poor substitute for experimental identification of exact causes. Joseph Lister rejected the Lancets' call for statistics about his successes and failures with antiseptic surgery and instead succeeded in persuading the medical community through a single dramatic case. Caramazza and his colleagues conclude—with Bernard, Lister, Freud, and the nineteenth-century tradition in neuropsychology— that individuals should be studied and generalizations about the mind drawn from the patterns they severally exhibit. The nineteenth-century neuropsychological tradition paid little heed to statistics, but this is the century of probability, and the revival of cognitive neuropsychology in our time made a clash with statistical methods almost inevitable.

12.2   An Inexhaustive Review

In one of the most articulate statements of the objection to group data, Caramazza and McCloskey say that they assume the following:

1. Normal cognitive performance (O) is the result of the activity of a set of processing components, which together comprise a cognitive system, M.
2. Impaired cognitive performance (O^*) reflects the activity of a functionally lesioned cognitive system, that is $M + L \rightarrow O^*$.
3. Basic research activity in cognitive neuropsychology involves determining, for any patient (P) whether or not there is an appropriate modification of a cognitive system—that is a functional lesion—which would account for the observed pattern of impaired cognitive performance. (1988, 520)

Their argument involves a diagram illustrating the (abnormal) outcomes (O_i^*) of a cognitive test (C) applied to various patients (P_i) who may be judged to share a "syndrome." In the equations below, M represents the normal cognitive organizations, while L_i represents the damage to that structure suffered by patient P_i. Consider now the case for research with brain-damaged patients. The following equations are a schematic representation of a group of patients.

P_1: $M + C + L_1 \rightarrow O_1^*$

P_2: $M + C + L_2 \rightarrow O_2^*$

P_3: $M + C + L_3 \rightarrow O_3^*$

P_i: $M + C + L_i \rightarrow O_i^*$

P_n: $M + C + L_n \rightarrow O_n^*$

Averaging performance O_1^* through O_n^* would be justified if we could assume that Ms, Cs, and Ls are equivalent in relevant respects for patients P_1 through P_n. We have already expressed our willingness to accept the assumption that Ms and Cs are equivalent. We cannot do the same, however, for the Ls—these are not under the control of the experimenter. It is an empirical matter to be decided by careful analysis whether or not any set of functional lesions are equivalent. In other words, in our research with brain-damaged patients we begin with the presumption that these patients have abnormal cognitive systems, and we may legitimately average their performance if and only if we have demonstrated empirically that the patients have equivalent functional lesions. (Caramazza and McCloskey 1988, 522–523)

Most of the critical responses to this and related demonstrations treat the argument as straightforward but fallacious. A long list of psychologists have offered rebuttals. Some of the responses involve obvious changes in the point of inquiry—from finding the structure and functions of cognitive parts to merely collecting data (Kosslyn and Intriligator 1992; Zurif, Swinney, and Fodor 1990), recourse to grand philosophical claims about the vanity of science (Zurif, Swinney, and Fodor 1990), and arguments about the difficulties of reliable measurement in individuals *without* group data (Bates, McDonald, MacWhinney, and Appelbaum 1991.) However important the latter claims are to methodology, they are irrelevant responses to the argument Caramazza, McCloskey, and others give about the unreliability of inference *with* group data. If both arguments were sound, the right conclusion would be that there can be no cognitive neuropsychological science.

Appealing to unspecified principles of philosophy of science rather than to any details of experimental design, Zurif, Swinney, and Fodor (1990) have objected that the argument must be unsound, for otherwise it would invalidate all of experimental psychology. Shallice (1988), who alone among the commentators gives the issue some statistical structure, also claims that, were it sound, standard pieces of experimental psychology would be invalid. A common response is to describe some statistical study that purports to establish something about the structure of mind. In effect, these examples say, "Look here, what's wrong with *this* use of group data?" For their side, Caramazza, McCloskey, and their colleagues have in turn attacked these examples.

The irrelevance of most of the rebuttals in defense of group data suggests that the argument against group studies is *not* very clear after all. With typical succinctness, Martha Farah has reformulated the argument of Caramazza and McCloskey in a few sentences:

Traditional neuropsychological group study designs ... are not appropriate for answering most questions about cognitive processes: These groups will be heterogeneous with respect to the impairments that are the subject of study, and we therefore risk basing our conclusions on average performance profiles that are artifactual, in that they may not exist in any one case. (1990, 145)

Farah's point is that if data are aggregated, we cannot identify individual profiles of the sort discussed in the previous chapter. Whether that is so, and what it implies, depends on how the data are aggregated. There are essentially only two ways to aggregate data on incapacities by syndrome: We may, for a sample population with the syndrome, record the individual profiles and report the frequency of each profile, or in other terms, *the joint frequency* of the possible incapacities. Alternatively, we may record for a sample the frequency of one incapacity, then record for the same sample (or another sample of subjects with the same syndrome) the frequency of another, distinct, incapacity, and so on. The second procedure records the *marginal frequency* of each incapacity, but does not tell us how often sets of incapacities occur together. Arguably, the second sort of aggregation is more typical. One study of a group of Wernicke aphasics may test them for one incapacity, while other studies of the same or other groups of Wernicke aphasics test for other incapacities, and the joint frequencies of incapacities are never investigated.

In principle, group studies that report the joint frequency of a set of possible incapacities tell us exactly as much as do individual studies, and they admit the same kind of learning-in-the-limit analysis offered in the previous chapter for individual studies. Group studies that report only marginal frequencies are more interesting.

12.3   Problems of Discovery from Frequencies with Deterministic Input/Output Behavior

Consider the problem of identifying normal structure from data that consists, not of the abnormal profiles observed, but only of the marginal frequency of observed incapacities. Recall the six graphs of the previous chapter (figure 12.1). Graph 2 implies that whenever incapacity $\langle I_1, O_1 \rangle$ occurs, either incapacity $\langle I_1, O_2 \rangle$ or incapacity $\langle I_2, O_1 \rangle$ or both must occur. Hence, necessarily, the frequency of the first incapacity cannot be greater than the sum of the frequencies of the later two incapacities minus the frequency of their joint occurrence. That is,

(1) $\mathrm{fr}(\sim\langle I_1, O_1 \rangle) \le \mathrm{fr}(\sim\langle I_1, O_2 \rangle)) + \mathrm{fr}(\sim\langle I_2, O_1 \rangle) - \mathrm{fr}(\sim\langle I_1, O_2 \rangle)$
       $\&\sim\langle I_2, O_1 \rangle)$

Therefore,

(2) $\mathrm{fr}(\sim\langle I_1, O_1 \rangle) \le \mathrm{fr}(\sim\langle I_1, O_2 \rangle)) + \mathrm{fr}(\sim\langle I_2, O_1 \rangle)$

Here the $\sim$ before a capacity indicates the absence of that capacity. Inequality (2) is, of course, vacuous if $\mathrm{fr}(\sim\langle I_1, O_2 \rangle)) + \mathrm{fr}(\sim\langle I_2, O_1 \rangle) \ge 1$.

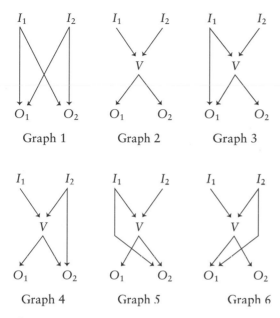

Graph 1 Graph 2 Graph 3

Graph 4 Graph 5 Graph 6

Figure 12.1

Graph 2 implies a constraint of the form (2) for each of the four capacities, that is:

(3) $\text{fr}(\sim\langle I_1, O_2\rangle) \le \text{fr}(\sim\langle I_1, O_1\rangle)) + \text{fr}(\sim\langle I_2, O_2\rangle)$

(4) $\text{fr}(\sim\langle I_2, O_1\rangle) \le \text{fr}(\sim\langle I_1, O_1\rangle)) + \text{fr}(\sim\langle I_2, O_2\rangle)$

(5) $\text{fr}(\sim\langle I_2, O_2\rangle) \le \text{fr}(\sim\langle I_1, O_2\rangle)) + \text{fr}(\sim\langle I_2, O_1\rangle)$

Each of graphs 3, 4, 5, and 6 will imply a distinct set of three of these four inequalities ((2) to (5)). For the alternative gating in which a capacity is intact if any path in the normal graph from input to output remains intact, all graphs except graph 1 imply all four inequalities.

The upshot is that under the conditions in which data on frequencies of incapacities are often obtained, there is a good case against trying to infer features of normal structure from the frequencies of individual incapacities. In our simple example, any structure is *consistent* with any set of marginal frequencies. If one assumes that models that *imply* observed inequalities like those above are true, rather than models that are merely consistent with the inequalities but do not imply them and one assumes that normal capacities are removed by the destruction of any pathway, then if one is lucky in the frequencies with which incapacities occur (and lucky as well that graph 1 is not the true structure), then five of the hypotheses about normal structure may be distinguished. If one assumes that normal capacities are only removed by destroying all pathways, then with the same assumptions and the same luck, one can infer only that there is an intermediate unobserved node ("V") in the normal structure. Either way, these are a lot of assumptions and a lot of luck.

The proposal of Bates et al. (1991) that cognitive neuropsychology rely on the maximum-likelihood principle might be understood as a preference for the graphs that entail observed inequalities among the frequencies over graphs that are merely consistent with the observed inequalities. So, on finding all four inequalities that graph 2 entails, we should prefer graph 2 to the other five graphs. The difficulty with the proposal is that no singular or unlikely event is necessary for other graphs to be true and accommodate the frequencies. The proposal, in effect, says that no credence should be given to that possibility.

12.4   Problems of Discovery with Indeterministic Input/Output Relations

Suppose that classification of responses as normal or abnormal is an imperfect indication of brain damage. There is a (high) probability that people without lesions will give the normal response, but also a (small) probability that people with lesions will give the normal response. The derivations of the inequalities of the previous section now no longer hold. Relations of statistical dependence take their place. Thus graph 2 requires that an incapacity in $\langle I_1, O_1 \rangle$ and the set of incapacities $\{\langle I_1, O_2 \rangle, \langle I_2, O_1 \rangle\}$ be statistically dependent, since in graph 2, once more, every lesion that removes a pathway in $\langle I_1, O_1 \rangle$ removes a pathway in one of the two capacities in the set. Graph 1 allows the dependency but does not require it.

A typical strategy in group studies is to compare average performance on a cognitive skill in a group of subjects selected for a combination of performance deficits (a syndrome) with the average performance of groups of normals for the same skill. In effect, the strategy is to find correlations, or statistical dependencies, among incapacities. The strategy seems to rely on the same principles as those discussed in the previous sections, but with statistical dependencies in place of strict inequalities. With luck, the strategy can falsify some of the six graphs; with the likelihood principle, the strategy can yield a preference for some graphs over others but cannot establish their truth.

Solutions to the problem of identifying mental structure in this case depend, then, either on luck or on stronger assumptions connecting lesions and the probability distribution of the data.

Assume that the probability of a response associated with an output node depends only on the state of the modules feeding directly into that output node. Then graphs of mental functioning have a Markov property. For example, for graph 2,

$$\mathrm{pr}(O_1 \mid I_1) = \sum_v \mathrm{pr}(O_1 \mid V) \cdot \mathrm{pr}(V \mid I_1)$$

Here the sum is take over all states v of the intermediate node V and we assume that the inputs are mutually exclusive. A similar condition can be imposed when inputs and responses are continuous, or when input values are discretely valued and responses are continuous. In any of these cases, the problem looks like standard psychometrics for normal subjects. For example, if the inputs are randomized and it is assumed that all of the influences are linear with independent noises, each normal graph and each lesioned subgraph determine characteristic constraints on the correlations. Graph 2, again, then requires the following:

$$\rho_{I_1, O_1} \rho_{I_2, O_2} = \rho_{I_1, O_2} \rho_{I_2, O_1}$$

Here ρ is the correlation coefficient for the subscripted pair of variables. None of the other normal graphs entails this condition, but subgraphs of graphs 3 to 6 will do so. So graph 2 could be identified from normals.

13

The Explanatory Power of Lesioning Neural Nets

13.1 Introduction

In recent years a number of neural-net or "connectionist" models have been proposed to explain both normal cognitive behavior and the cognitive characteristics of patients who, through brain damage, have lost some normal capacities. Typically, a network model is developed that generates some symbolic representation of the normal capacity; subsequently, some set of network nodes, links, or both are removed to generate a representation of the capacities of a brain-damaged subject or subjects. The "lesioned" network may or may not be retrained.[1] Messaro (1988) objects that for every conceivable behavior, there is some connectionist model able to explain it, and thus according to a common methodological perspective, no general connectionist hypothesis is supported by the phenomena. The same objection was raised against Farah's (1994) illustrations of lesioned neural-net explanations of neuropsychological data.

The force of such objections can be given a Bayesian cast. Suppose it is shown that, with proper adjustment of free parameters, a certain theory can accommodate any possible empirical phenomena. Let π be the unique vector of parameter values for T that, with T, is consistent with and entails E. Then $\mathrm{pr}(E \mid T) = \mathrm{pr}(\pi \mid T)$, and therefore:

$$\mathrm{pr}(T \mid E) = \mathrm{pr}(E \mid T) \cdot \mathrm{pr}(T)/\mathrm{pr}(E) = \mathrm{pr}(\pi \mid T) \cdot \mathrm{pr}(T)/\mathrm{pr}(E)$$

If, now, $\mathrm{pr}(\pi \mid T) = \mathrm{pr}(E)$, which seems the only plausible prior probability distribution for parameters in a theory that can accommodate all possible data, it follows that $\mathrm{pr}(T \mid E) = \mathrm{pr}(T)$ and no data can confirm T.

The objection raises a set of methodological questions about neural nets and cognitive neuropsychology. Neural-net models have a representation of behavior as input/output functions, or more generally, as probability distributions on observable nodes. A damaged-brain neural-net model is really two models representing two behavior sets, one normal and one injured, related by the fact that the abnormal model is a lesioned, and possibly retrained, version of the normal model.

1. Under what conditions is the objection true or false? Think of alternative assumptions about neural nets as defining various classes of models. Which classes have the property that they are *universal*, that is, after lesioning and retraining, they can generate all mathematically possible pairs of behavioral representations each of which is representable singly?

2. If a class of models is not universal, how can counterexamples to the class be recognized?

3. If a model class is not universal, is it possible to learn from empirical data (for example, by Bayesian inference or some other method) whether it is true, and if so, under what assumptions is such learning possible?

4. Within which model classes is it possible to falsify, or at least to falsify in the limit with increasing data, a particular normal hypothesis by observing abnormal behavior?

5. Correspondingly, within which model classes is it possible to falsify, or at least to falsify in the limit with increasing data, a particular normal hypothesis by observing abnormal behavior?

In what follows, I answer some of these questions for certain classes of neural-net models. The classes for which results can be shown do not correspond neatly to the divisions among models used in the neural-net literature, but they are recognizable versions of neural-net assumptions. I note some difficult open questions and some issues about alternative reconstructions of neural-net statistics. I will give no proofs, since the results described below are simply applications of theorems in the statistical and computer-science literature on directed graphs and probabilities.

13.2   Networks and Graphs

The neural nets we will be concerned with represent behavioral patterns as probability relations over nodes or vertices that in turn represent cognitive stimuli or responses. The net determines a probability distribution over the values of a collection of nodes, each node thought of as a system that can take varied values. Some of the nodes, and their values, represent actions or behavior that is measured in some setting, some experiment. The total probability distribution on all of the nodes and their possible values is related to the probability relations between network nodes. Think of the nodes as cognitive parts, and imagine a node *A* with several inputs and a single output, as below:

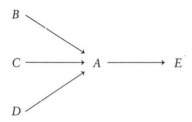

Assume for the time being that that there is no feedback loop from *E* to *B*, *C*, or *D*, and that there is no further node that influences both *A* and *B* or both *A* and *C*. If all of the links between *B*, *C*, and *A* are broken and *B*, *C* have no direct or indirect links with *D*, variation in *B*, *C* will produce no variation in *A*.

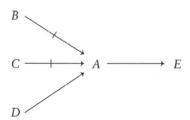

A may then vary spontaneously or, through its link with *D*, because *D* varies, but *A* does not vary because of any connection with *B* and *C*. In this case, observing *B* or *C* or both should tell us nothing about *A*. In probabilistic terms, the probability of any value of *A*, given values of *B* and *C*, would just equal the probability of that value of *A* without the information about *B* or *C*: $\mathrm{pr}(A \mid B, C) = \mathrm{pr}(A)$. The absence of any causal relation between parts is directly reflected in the independence of probabilities of states of those parts.

Suppose that in the unbroken condition, B, C, D influence E only through A and there is no node that influences both E and any of B, C, or D. Then if A or all the links into A or all the links out of A are broken, B, C, D will be independent of E: $\text{pr}(E \mid B, C, D) = \text{pr}(E)$. What about the unbroken condition? Since B, C, and D influence E only through A and nothing influences both E and B, C, or D, if we know the value of A at any moment, knowing the value of the B, C, D that helped to produce that value of A will tell us nothing further about the value of E (at any time). If we do an experiment in which B, C, D are varied as we wish and then the values of A and of E are measured for each distinct state imposed on B, C, D, the values of E will be independent of the values of B, C, D conditional on the values of A, that is, $\text{pr}(E \mid B, C, D, A) = \text{pr}(E \mid A)$. E is conditionally independent of B, C, D given A. Such independencies can be verified in feedforward nets with any of the activation functions commonly used.

The sorts of neural networks we are discussing can be thought of as directed graphs whose nodes are variables that can take different values and have a joint probability distribution on all of their possible values. The remarks in the previous two paragraphs indicate that not just any probability distribution can be coupled with just any (acyclic) directed graph corresponding to a feedforward network. The connectivity structure of a network implies restrictions, in the form of independence and conditional-independence requirements, on any probability distribution associated with the network. Recurrent networks correspond to directed graphs containing a cycle. I will formalize this idea and address some of the questions posed above first for feedforward networks and then for recurrent networks.

13.3   Feedforward Networks as Bayes Nets

Our first problem is to state in a general and precise way the restrictions on probability given by a network structure in feedforward networks.

We require some preliminary definitions. A directed graph is a pair, **V**, **E**, where **E** is a set of ordered pairs (directed edges) of members of nonempty **V** (vertices). A member of **E** will be represented as $A \rightarrow B$. For an undirected graph, **E** is a set of unordered pairs (undirected edges). For a mixed graph, **E** may contain both directed and undirected edges. For a directed edge $A \rightarrow B$, A is the *tail* of the edge and B is the *head*; the edge is *out of* A and *into* B, and A is a *parent* of B and B is a *child* of A. A sequence of edges $\langle E_1, \ldots, E_n \rangle$ in a graphical object G is an *undirected path* if and only if there exists a sequence of vertices $\langle V_1, \ldots, V_{n+1} \rangle$ such that E_i has endpoints V_i and V_{i+1}. A path U is *acyclic* if no vertex appears more than once in the corresponding sequence of vertices. We will assume that an undirected path is acyclic unless specifically mentioned otherwise. A sequence of edges $\langle E_1, \ldots, E_n \rangle$ in G is a *directed path D from* V_1 *to* V_n if and only if there exists a sequence of vertices $\langle V_1, \ldots, V_{n+1} \rangle$ such that for $1 < i < n$, there is a directed edge $V_i \rightarrow V_{i+1}$ on D. If there is an acyclic directed path from A to B or $B = A$, then A is an *ancestor* of B, and B is a *descendant* of A. If $\mathbf{Z}$ is a set of variables, A is an *ancestor* of $\mathbf{Z}$ if and only if it is an ancestor of a member of $\mathbf{Z}$, and similarly for *descendants*. A directed graph is *acyclic* if and only if it contains no directed cyclic paths. A vertex V is a *collider* on an undirected path U if and only if U contains a pair of distinct edges adjacent on the path and into V. Vertices X, Y in a directed graph are *d-separated* by a set $\mathbf{Z}$ (not containing X or Y) of vertices if and only if every undirected path between X, Y either contains a noncollider in $\mathbf{Z}$ or a collider having no descendant in $\mathbf{Z}$. If X, Y are not d-separated by $\mathbf{Z}$, then they are said to be *d-connected, given* $\mathbf{Z}$. The notions of d-separation and d-connection are due to Judea Pearl (1988).

Let us give the connections between nodes in neural networks a slightly more definite form. Assume that the state of each node X in a network G may be written as (1):

(1) $X = F_X(Y_1, \ldots, Y_n, \varepsilon_X)$

Here the Y_i are nodes in the network with edges directed into X—the parents of X in the network—and ε_X is not a node variable but a noise term with positive variance. All noise terms are jointly statistically independent, and each noise term ε_X is jointly independent of all variables (nodes) that are not descendants of X in G. Further assume that for some range of values of the error terms, the set of all equations (1) have a simultaneous solution. Then the equations and the probability distribution on the error terms determine a joint probability distribution on the nodes of the graph. I will sometimes refer to functions such as F_X as *transmission functions*.

I assume that lesioning a network and perhaps retraining may alter the transmission functions, but also that the compositions of those functions are determined by the respective topologies of the normal and lesioned networks. The results that follow can be found in Spirtes et al. 1993, 2001.

Theorem 1   Let G be a directed acyclic graph. Let G^* be an extension of G that contains, for each vertex X in G, a vertex ε_X (error for X) of zero indegree and unit outdegree adjacent to X, and let P be a joint probability distribution of positive variance on the vertices of G^*, and let F_X be the transmission function (measurable with respect to P) for vertex X. For all nodes U, V and all sets $\mathbf{Z}$ of nodes in a directed acyclic graph (whose nodes are related by transmission functions such as (1)), if P is a joint probability distribution on the noise terms, with positive variance making all noise terms jointly independent, then U is independent of V given $\mathbf{Z}$ if $\mathbf{Z}$ d-separates U, V.

A subnetwork, or subgraph, of G is any graph obtained by deleting in G edges or nodes (and edges adjacent to those nodes) or both. The following result is elementary (Spirtes et al. 1993, 2000):

Theorem 2   If U, V are d-separated by $\mathbf{Z}$ in a directed acyclic graph G, then they are d-separated by $\mathbf{Z}$ in every subgraph of G containing them.

These theorems mean that the connectivity of a feedforward net may imply various independence facts, no matter what the form of the transmission function between nodes—no matter, that is, whether F is additive, sigmoid, etc. And further, lesioning such a network cannot eliminate any of these independencies.

13.4   Feedforward Networks without Unobserved Nodes

For this class of network models, deleting any edge or vertex (and therefore edges into or out of that vertex) results in a network that, however trained and parameterized, will generate at least one conditional-independence relation that does not hold in the original network.

Theorem 3   For any acyclic network G faithfully parameterized by functions such as (1) with independent noises and any network G' whose topology is a subgraph of G and that is parameterized by functions such as (1) with independent noises, an independence or conditional-independence relation holds for G' that does not hold for G.

I will say that an *oracle* for independence is a procedure that responds with the correct answer to any query about the independence or conditional independence of variables represented by observed nodes in a network. I will say that an *asymptotic oracle* is a procedure that responds to any such query and sample data with answers that converge in probability to the correct answer as the sample size increases without bound. For example, for Gaussian-distributed variables, an asymptotic oracle can be fashioned by systematically reducing the significance level as sample size increases in tests for vanishing correlations or partial correlations. Now some of the questions posed in section 13.1 can be answered:

1–2. Given an oracle, the class is refuted by any normal/damaged pair of probability distributions in which every independence or conditional-independence relation in the damaged distribution holds in the normal distribution.

3. Given a linear ordering of the (noninput and nonoutput) nodes, for example, a time ordering, the network structure can be uniquely determined from the facts of independence and conditional independence.

4–5. For any hypothesis (in this class) about normal networks, there is a probability distribution that, if observed in brain damaged subjects, would refute the hypotheses.

Question 3 has a more complicated answer, which we will not consider here, when an ordering of the nodes is not known.

13.5 Hidden Nodes

A probability distribution on the nodes of a network may imply independence facts that are not guaranteed by the network structure. Extra independencies will arise, for example, if there are two pathways, one excitory and one inhibitory, from a node U to a node V whose influences on V *exactly* cancel one another. We say a distribution P is *faithful* to a directed graph G if there are no extra independencies of this kind, that is, if every conditional independence P corresponds to a d-separation fact about G. It has been shown that when the functions F in (1) are linear, almost all distributions corresponding to a given graph are faithful, or in other terms, that for parameter values giving an unfaithful distribution, almost any arbitrarily small variation in parameter values will result in a faithful distribution (Spirtes et al. 1993, 2000). A parallel result holds when the functions F are stochastic, the error terms are eliminated, and each node has a finite set of possible values. Faithfulness may be viewed as a kind of stability requirement, for the almost any variation in the parameters of an unfaithful network would eliminate some probabilistic independence or conditional independence (although small deviations from independence would only be revealed in large samples).

A common assumption about explanations is that, other things equal, explanations that necessitate extra parameters and perfect cancellations are to be abjured when alternative explanations without these features are available and are otherwise as good. So far as reliable inference is concerned, a methodological preference of this kind is an assumption about how the world is not. So we have:

Assumption 1   The probability distribution associated with the neural network of the brain is faithful to that network.

From the assumption and the two theorems (and on the assumption that lesions break edges), it follows immediately that any independencies or conditional independencies in a probability distribution for a network representing normal structure must also be present in any probability distribution obtained by lesioning and retraining the network. Of course, a lesioned network can exhibit further independencies not exhibited by the normal network. In one reasonably clear sense, the claim that lesioning neural nets can simulate any imaginable pairing of normal and abnormal behavior is false.

13.6   Recurrent Networks

The case of recurrent networks—or, equivalently, networks with feedback or networks represented by cyclic directed graphs—is more complicated. We continue to assume that a node is influenced by its parent nodes according to a function of form (1). Suppose that we make the following unrealistic assumption:

Assumption 2   All transmission functions F are linear.

In the case of assumption 2, Spirtes (1993, 1995) has shown that theorem 1 applies to cyclic graphs as well as to acyclic networks. Theorem 2 applies as well, and Assumption 1 makes as much sense here as for acyclic graphs. So we again have the result that there are mathematically possible normal behaviors that can be represented by a linear recurrent network—a cyclic graph—G, and there are similarly conceivable abnormal behaviors that can be represented by a linear recurrent network H, but for no G and H representing the probability distributions of the normal and abnormal behaviors can H be obtained by lesioning G.

In nonlinear recurrent systems, conditional independence does not neatly correspond to lesioning. But a generalization of theorem 1 shows that the independence implications of nonlinear cyclic networks can be obtained by (1) transforming a strongly connected component (a set of vertices each of which is the ancestor of all others) into a clique, (2) adding edges from the parent of any vertex in the cycle to all vertices in the component, (3) applying d-separation (Spirtes 1993, 1995). Faithfulness and assumption 1 make sense as before, and under those assumptions we again have the result that there are pairs of patterns of independence and conditional-independence relations that cannot be reproduced as a normal net and its lesioned subnet.

13.7 Implications

The application of directed graphical models to this methodological issue is potentially more than an oddity. Brain events can now be recorded by a variety of physical techniques, including evoked-response potentials, functional magnetic resonance imaging, etc. Characterizations of the equivalence classes of graphical representations implying the same conditional-independence relations invite the design of algorithms that will use the outcomes of tests for conditional independence to help reconstruct causal sequences of brain events during and after various cognitive tasks. Algorithms for the acyclic case are already available and implemented in several programs, for example, the TETRAD programs, (Scheines et al. 1994). Richardson (1994) has characterized graphical d-separation equivalence for cyclic graphs, and under the assumption outlined in previous sections, he has found a feasible algorithm that uses conditional-independence facts to construct the equivalence class of cyclic graphs for linearly related variables. While there is no reason to think the dependencies among brain events are linearly related, as in other areas linear approximations may be very useful. And the d-separation property, while provably necessary in the linear case, remains a reasonable assumption for nonlinear recurrent networks. Still needed are algorithms that, as in the acyclic cases, are correct and complete even when unmeasured common causes may be influencing two or more recorded variables, and a theory of equivalence and search for the nonlinear case.

It may well be, however, that recurrent neural nets are better modeled by time series than by the finite cyclic graphs conventionally used to represent them. The relations between the two representations, both used widely in econometrics, are little understood.[2]

IV

Psychometrics and Social Psychology

14

Social Statistics and Genuine Inquiry: The Case of *The Bell Curve*

14.1 Introduction

Herrnstein and Murray's *The Bell Curve* (1994) put American academic social scientists—economists, epidemiologists, sociologists, social psychologists—in an uncomfortable place. The conclusions of the book are unwelcome, while the methods of the book appear to be the standbys of everyday social science. The unstated problem for many commentators is how to reject the particular conclusions of *The Bell Curve* without also rejecting the larger enterprises of statistical social science, psychometrics, and social psychology. The hard issue is whether the methods of large parts of social science are bogus, phony, pseudoscientific. They are. The other hard issue is whether there are better methods attempted to the important tasks of social science. There are.

14.2 Varieties of Pseudoscience

Pseudoscience comes in a lot of varieties, not equally irremediable. The cold fusion episode represents one sort of pseudoscience, the sort in which competent, serious scientists step outside of their range of expertise and make unskillful and incompetent use of techniques that others more expert can and do use reliably to address the same questions. Astrology is quite another sort of pseudoscience, the sort that has a technology that no one—not even the greatest astrologer—can reliably use to gain useful information, because it is premised on radically false claims. There is a third kind of pseudoscience, of which no exact historical examples come to mind (determinations of atomic weights in chemistry from 1810 to 1860 or so was something like this), characterized by techniques that work reliably only in rare domains but are used much more widely, where they succeed, if at all, only by chance. The first employment of the young Leibniz, later a discoverer of the calculus, illustrates a fourth kind of pseudoscience. Leibniz was charged with devising a proof that a certain person, and no other, should be selected for a political office, a proof that Leibniz completed some years after the selection had been made. In Leibniz's kind of political science, methods are designed and applied with the intention of justifying prefixed conclusions. Conclusions drive inquiry rather than inquiry conclusions. Leibniz's example is only the extreme of a range of cases in which data are not permitted to speak freely.

Besides all these, there is a kind of metapseudoscience that, without proof, declares vast terrains of inquiry ever beyond exploration by any scientific method. J. M. Dumas was the most influential French chemist of the middle of the nineteenth century—his textbook is still in print in France—and he ruled that the atomic composition of matter is unknowable. If he were master, he wrote, the word *atom* would be banned from chemistry because it presupposes something beyond all experience. Dumas's view was not that atomism was false or nonsensical; he *knew* it was unknowable. At the end of the nineteenth century the great German physical chemist W. Ostwald held the same opinion. In the middle of the twentieth century B. F. Skinner ruled that whatever mental phenomena intervene between stimulus and response are unknowable— no doubt something goes on in between, but no scientific method could discover what. Critics rightly pointed out that strict behaviorism was an elaborate self-deception: as if to defy Descartes's "Cogito, ergo sum," John Watson, the first American behaviorist, went so far as to claim that there are no minds. In practice, behaviorists everywhere attributed inner states to people and creatures, and used those attributions in the design and assessment of their experiments. They were forsworn, nonetheless, from actually thinking about what they were doing, and so from any chance of doing it better. Karl Pearson's legacy in statistics is much the same. Pearson wrote perhaps the most silly influential book of philosophy ever published, *The Grammar of Science* (1911), in which he maintained, repeatedly and without any sense of incongruity, that there is no material world, the entire world is nothing but subjective sensation, and sensation is the production of *brains*. He coupled an acute critical sense with a wonderful tolerance for conceptual incoherence, nowhere more damaging than in his strong convictions about particular causal relations (the hereditary causes of virtue—Pearson was a keen eugenicist) incongruously coupled with his equally strong conviction that causation is nothing but correlation, so that in his judgement Yule's and Spearman's searches for structure behind data were vain efforts deserving the scorn he gave them. *The Grammar of Science* is still the semiofficial philosophy of some professional statisticians, and the opinions of several contemporary eminences seem close to Pearson's.

Almost unanimously, social scientists criticizing *The Bell Curve* have treated the book as a cold fusion episode, in which people who should have known better used the competent methods of the social sciences—factor analysis, regression, and logistic regression—incompetently. I have read any number of perfectly sound criticisms of this sort, and yet I think they do not refute, but only repress, the terrible thought that *The Bell Curve* signals something fundamentally wrong with much of contemporary social science: that social-scientific methods are like those of early nineteenth-century chemists, used widely but reliable only in special cases, and that the standard of argument in social science is Leibnizian. Part of what troubles me about the cold-fusion simile is that parallel criticisms could be, and have been, made of many celebrated pieces of empirical social science: the arguments that smoking causes lung cancer were soundly ridiculed by statistically sophisticated critics; econometric reanalysis of the influence of lead exposure on children's IQ failed to find any significant effect when reasonable measurement error was allowed; the regression model of the *American Occupational Structure*, cited by the National Academy of Science as *primo* social science, fails almost any statistical test, and so on. What troubles me more is that the principal methods of causal analysis used in *The Bell Curve* and throughout the social sciences are either provably unreliable in the circumstances in which they are commonly used or are of unknown reliability. But I'm getting ahead of the story.

14.3   Inquiry and Discovery

Philosophical skepticism trades on two maneuvers: a focus on the worst case and a demand that any method of forming belief find the truth in all logically possible circumstances. When action must be taken, skepticism is in league with obscurantism and know-nothingism and stands in opposition to forces that are more optimistic about the information that inquiry can provide to judgement. In the last century the principal tool of scientific optimism—although not always of social optimism—was social statistics. Social statistics promised something less than a method of inquiry that is reliable in every possible circumstance, but something more than sheer ignorance; it promised methods that, under explicit and often plausible assumptions, but not in every logically possible circumstance, converge to the truth, whatever that may be—methods whose liability to error in the short run can be quantified and measured.

That promise was kept for three important statistical enterprises—experimental design, hypothesis testing, and parameter estimation—which for decades were the cynosure of professional statistical study, but it failed in the important parts of social inquiry that decide which parameters to estimate and which hypotheses to test when full experimental control, or at least randomization of putative causes, is unavailable. To make those decisions with the same guarantee of conditional reliability requires methods of search and theoretical inquiries into the reliabilities of those methods. Social statistics produced and used a variety of procedures—factor analysis and regression are the principal examples—for searching for appropriate hypotheses, but no analysis of the conditions for their reliability. The reasons their reliabilities were insufficiently analyzed and alternative methods not sought are complex. They have to do with a positivism that, to this day, grips much of social statistics, and that holds that causal hypotheses are intrinsically unscientific. Since almost all hypotheses of social inquiry are causal, this opinion requires a certain mental flexibility that inquiry into the reliabilities of methods of search for causal hypotheses would surely complicate. Perhaps an equally important reason that reliabilities were not sufficiently analyzed is the view that causal hypotheses are theories, and theories are the special prerogative of experts, not of algorithms. These prejudices combined with a number of more technical disciplinary issues. For example, search methods are difficult to associate with any uniform measure of uncertainty analogous to the standard-error function for a parameter estimator, and social scientists and social statisticians have come to demand such measures without reflection. Again, disciplines are usually blind to their history, and although causal questions motivated much of the development of statistics, the paradigmatic tool for mathematical analysis in statistics is the theory of probability—there is no formal language in the subject for causal analysis (Pearl 2000). In some measure this state of affairs has been abetted by philosophy of science, which for generations taught that there could be no principles, no "logic," to scientific discovery.

The incoherence between practice and methodological theory would do little harm were the methods of searching for causal hypotheses that have developed in social statistics, and that are widely taught to psychologists and social scientists and widely used to justify conclusions, reliable under conditions that might reasonably be assumed in the various domains to which the search methods are applied. They are not. We are left with enterprises that use the most rigorous possible methods to estimate parameters in causal models that are often produced by whimsy, prejudice, demonstrably unreliable search procedures, or, often without admission, ad hoc search methods that are sometimes reliable, sometimes not.

There is a remedy. Clear representations by directed graphs of causal hypotheses, and their statistical implications, in train with rigorous investigation of search procedures, have been developed in the last decade in a thinly populated intersection of computer science, statistics, and philosophy. The empirical results obtained with these methods, including a number of cases in which the causal predictions were independently confirmed, have been good, perhaps surprisingly good.

14.4 *The Bell Curve*

The Bell Curve is distinguished from a thousand and more efforts at non- or semi- or quasi-experimental social science and social psychology chiefly by its length, popular style, ambition, and conclusions. The statistical methods of the book are multiple regression, logistic regression, and factor analysis—techniques routinely taught to psychology and social science students in almost every graduate program in these subjects and routinely applied to make causal inferences from data of every kind. Most social samples are convenience samples, not random samples. The methods and kinds of data of *The Bell Curve* are not very different in character from those in celebrated works of social statistics, for example, the regression analyses in Peter Blau and Otis Dudley Duncan's *The American Occupational Structure* or the factor analyses in Melvin Kohn's *Class and Conformity*; many statistical consultants use the same methods to guide business, military, and government policy on endless issues. One of the authors of *The Bell Curve*, Charles Murray, is a well-trained political scientist, and the other, Richard Herrnstein, was a prominent psychologist; these authors are not naïfs or incompetents.

When Herrnstein and Murray write "cause," I take them to mean cause—something that varies in the population and whose variation produces variation in other variables, something that, if we could intervene and alter, would alter something else we did not directly wiggle. When they say genes cause IQ scores, I take them to mean that if somehow we could alter the relevant distribution of genes in the population, without altering directly anything else—the "environment"—then a different distribution of IQ scores would result. That is how Ronald Fisher (1958) thought of the causal role of genes in producing phenotypes, and it is how we think of causation in most other contexts. Some statisticians, notably Paul Holland (1986), have claimed, contrary to Fisher, that it is nonsensical to talk of genes as causes. The thought seems to be that causation is a relation between individuals or between attributes of an individual, and I, for one, and you, for another, could not be who we are if our respective genetic structures were altered. The objection is wonderfully philosophical, Leibnizian even, though it harks to a different aspect of Leibniz's philosophy than his political proofs, but hardly persuasive in an age in which we can stick bits of DNA in chromosomes and reidentify the chromosome before and after the insertion.

There are two parts to the causal argument of *The Bell Curve*. One part argues that there is a feature of people, general intelligence, that is principally responsible for how people perform on IQ tests. The other part argues that this feature, as measured by IQ tests, causes a lot of other things. The first part is argued by appeal to factor analysis; the second part by appeal to regression. Because the hypotheses are causal, there is no substitute for making the causal claims explicit, and for that I will use graphical causal models. They explicitly represent important distinctions that are often lost when the discussion is couched in more typical formalisms.

14.5   Factor Analysis

Herrnstein and Murray rely on factor analytic studies to justify the claim that there is a single unobserved cause—which they, following Charles Spearman, call *g* for general intelligence—whose variation in the human population is responsible for most of the variation in scores on IQ tests. I want instead to consider the very idea of factor analysis as a reliable method for discovering the unobserved.

The issue is one of those delicate cases where it is important to say the right thing for the right reason. Stephen Jay Gould says the right thing about factor analysis—it is unreliable—but partly for the wrong reasons: that there exist alternative, distinct causal structures that are "statistically equivalent" and that entities and processes postulated because they explained observed correlations should not be "reified," that is, should not be taken seriously and literally. At the level of generality they are given, even if not intended, Gould's reasons would be the end of science, including his own. Atoms, molecules, gravitational fields, the orbits of the planets, even the reality of the past are all beyond the eye and earshot that led our scientific ancestors, and lead us still, to believe in them. Physicists and philosophers of science have known for much of this century that standard physical theories—Newtonian gravitational theory, for example—admit alternative theories with different entities that equally save the phenomena. An objection that, when applied even handedly, indicts factor analysis along with the best of our science leaves factor analysis in excellent company. The problems of factor analysis are more particular: the kinds of alternatives factor-analytic procedures allow, the kinds of restrictions the factor-analytic tradition employs to eliminate alternatives, and, in consequence, the want of correspondence between factor-analytic results and actual structures from which data are generated.

Herrnstein and Murray's history of factor analysis requires a correction. They say that Spearman introduced the concept of general intelligence upon noticing that scores on his "mental" tests were all strongly positively correlated. Not exactly. Spearman developed his argument in various roughly equivalent forms over half a century,[1] but it came down to the following. The correlations of any four mental test scores i, j, k, l satisfy three equations:

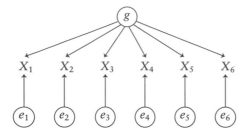

Figure 14.1

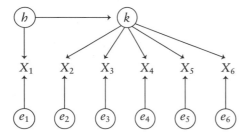

Figure 14.2

$$p_{ij}p_{kl} = p_{il}p_{jk} = p_{ik}p_{jl}$$

Spearman observed that these "tetrad" equations are implied by any linear structure in which scores on tests are all influenced by a single common cause, and otherwise sources of variation in test scores are uncorrelated. The graph is given in figure 14.1, where unobserved factors appear in circles.

Spearman realized that certain alternative structures would also generate the tetrad equations, for example, the graph in figure 14.2, but he thought of such structures as simply finer hypotheses about the structure of general intelligence, *g*.

Spearman must have known that structures with still more latent variables can account for the data. The tetrads, for example, can be made to vanish by suitable choice of the linear coefficients when there are two or more common latent factors affecting the measured variables. Such models might be rejected on the grounds that models that postulate fewer unobserved causes are more likely to be true than those that save the same phenomena by postulating more unobserved causes, but that

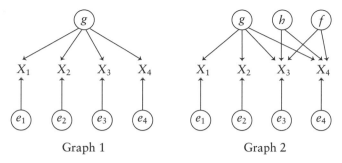

Figure 14.3

is a very strong assumption. A weaker one would serve the purpose: factor models assume that observed variables that do not influence one another are independent, conditional on all of their common causes—an assumption that is a special case of the Markov Assumption for directed graphical models. The rank constraints used in factor analysis—of which vanishing tetrads are a special case—are implied by conditional independencies in factor models, conditional independencies guaranteed by the topological structure of the graph of the model, no matter what values the linear coefficients or "factor loadings" may have. To exclude more latent variables when fewer will do, Spearman needed only to assume that vanishing tetrads do not depend on the constraints on the numerical values of the linear coefficients or "factor loadings," but are implied by the underlying causal structure. A general version of this second assumption has been called "faithfulness." It is known that the set of values of linear parameters (coefficients and variances) that generate probability distributions unfaithful to a directed graph is measure zero in the natural measure on parameter space.

To see the point, compare graphs 1 and 2 in figure 14.3. Let the factor loadings of g in graphs 1 and 2 be a_i, the factor loadings of h in graph 2 be b_i, and the factor loadings of f be c_i, where the index is over the measured variable connected to the factor. Then in graph 1 the vanishing tetrad differences follow from the commutativity of multiplication, that is, that $a_i a_j a_k a_l = a_i a_k a_j a_l$. In graph 2, however, the tetrad equation $\rho_{12}\rho_{34} = \rho_{13}\rho_{24}$ requires that $a_1 a_2 (a_3 a_4 + b_3 b_4 + c_3 c_4) = a_1 a_3 a_2 a_4$, that is, $b_3 b_4 = -c_3 c_4$.

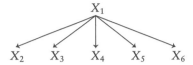

Figure 14.4

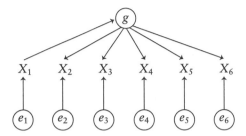

Figure 14.5

In the absence of further substantive assumptions, however, neither faithfulness nor the much stronger simplicity assumption would lead from tetrad constraints to Spearman's latent-common-cause models. Quite different structures also imply his tetrad equations, for example, the graph in figure 14.4, where I have omitted the error terms. The vanishing of all tetrads guarantees that a single common cause suffices; it doesn't guarantee that the common cause is unmeasured. Figures 14.1 and 14.4 are distinguished, however, by the vanishing partial correlations they require among measured variables: figure 14.1 requires none; figure 14.4 requires that all partials on X_1 vanish. But figure 14.5 cannot be distinguished from figure 14.1 by vanishing tetrads and vanishing partial correlations. So far as I know, Spearman and his followers never considered these matters.

Spearman's original mental tests did not prove well correlated with teachers' and others' judgements of intelligence, and they were replaced by tests in Binet and Simon's mode. These latter tests had more complicated correlation structures, and typically, all tetrads did not vanish. Spearman's followers, notably Karl Holzinger, began the practice of assuming a single common cause, g, and then introducing additional common causes as they were needed to account for residual correlation and prevent the implication of tetrad equations not approximated in the data. Their procedure guaranteed that if most of the correlation among measures could be attributed to one common cause, it would be, even if alternative structures and factor loadings were consistent with the data. Reliability was never an issue.[2]

Thurstone (1947) said he discovered factor analysis when he realized the tetrads were merely the determinant of a second-order minor. The mathematical idea in factor analysis is that the rank of the correlation matrix gives information about the minimum number of latent common causes needed to reproduce the matrix. The procedural idea is a method —the centroid method—of forming from the covariances a particular linear causal model in which all of the correlations of measured variables are due to latent common causes. Thurstone realized that the models his procedure produced were not the only possible linear-, latent-variable explanations of the data from which he started, and that in fact any nonsingular linear combination of latent factors obtained by his centroid method would do as well.

Thurstone's problem is fairly compared to John Dalton's. Thurstone had no means of uniquely determining the latent factor loadings and relations, and Dalton had no means of determining relative atomic weights. Both sought to remove or at least reduce underdetermination with a simplicity principle.[3] In graphical terms, Thurstone's proposal was to find the linear combination of latents that produces the fewest total number of directed edges from latent factors to measured variables. Thurstone thought such a "simple structure" is unique for each correlation matrix, but it is not. More important, why should we think actual mental structures obey Thurstone's rule of simplicity any more than atoms obey Dalton's? Unlike faithfulness, simple structure has no special measure-theoretic virtue and no special stability properties.

Thurstone's factor analysis rapidly displaced Spearman's methods. Reliability does not seem to have been one of the reasons. Guilford, who discusses both in his *Psychometric Methods*, recommends factor analysis over tetrad analysis on the grounds of computational tractability. Explicitly for Thurstone, and implicitly no doubt for many users of his method and its variants, factor analysis was a procedure for searching for latent causes. Thurstone has no theoretical means of establishing the reliability of such searches, which is no doubt motivation for his equivocations about the aims of factor analysis. Lacking a digital computer, he also had no means of testing the reliability of his search procedure on data produced from known structures. We do.

I understand the serious claims of factor-analytic psychometric studies to be (1) that there are a number of unmeasured features fixed in each person but continuously variable from person to person; (2) that these features have some causal role in the production of responses to questions on psychometric tests and the function giving the dependence of measured responses on unmeasured features is the same for all persons; (3) that variation of these features within the population causes the variation in response scores that members of the population would give were the entire population tested; (4) that some of these unmeasured features cause the production of responses to more than one test item; (5) that the correlations among test scores that would be found were the entire population tested is due entirely to those unmeasured features that influence two or more measured features. Suppose, for the moment, that we grant these psychometric assumptions. The reliability of factor analysis does not follow. For factor analysis to find the truth, a number of other conditions are necessary, including these: (6) the measured variables must be normally distributed, linear functions of their causes; (7) measurement of some features must not influence the measures found for other features, and neither the values of measured features nor the values of their unmeasured causes should influence whether a person is sampled; (8) two or more latent factors must not perfectly cancel the effects of one another on measured responses.

These conditions are necessary, but I doubt they are sufficient for any sort of factor analysis to yield the truth (in sufficiently large samples) about the number of factors, about what measured variables each latent factor influences, or about the strengths of those influences. So there are really two questions. First, when the eight assumptions just mentioned are granted, how reliable is factor analysis? And second, what credence should we give to the assumptions?

The rank of the population-correlation matrix gives the minimum number of variables n such that each measured variable can be written as a linear function of n variables plus random, independent error. In general, this is not the number of latent variables—for example, if some of the measured variables have a linear dependence on other measured variables. But when there are no measured-variable-to-measured-variable influences, the rank of the correlation matrix for the population tells us the minimum number of latent factors. Even so, on finite samples, factor analysis may fail either because the true structure does not minimize the number of latent variables or because of statistical or algorithmic artifacts. Computer simulation provides the best way I know to come to some understanding about the reliability of the methods on the given assumptions. Specify a number of alternative structures as directed graphs, identifying nodes as latent or measured. Specify means and variances for each of the exogenous variables (in graphical terms, variables of zero indegree), and for each directed edge specify a nonzero real number representing the corresponding linear coefficient. Then, for each such structure, calculate the correlation matrix of the measured variables, give the matrix to factor-analysis programs, and count the error rates of the procedures for the various features that factor analysis is supposed to reveal. Do the same again using the structures and a random-number generator to generate sample correlation matrices for samples of various sizes. I will at least illustrate what I have in mind with some simple examples of such graphs:

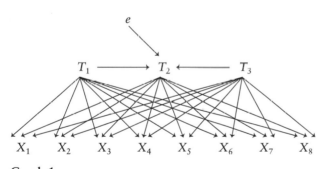

Graph 1

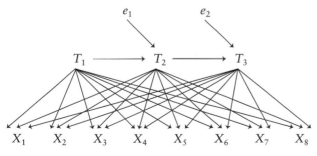

Graph 2

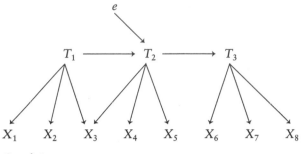

Graph 3

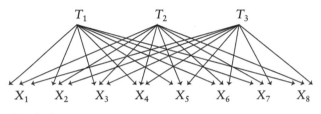

Graph 4

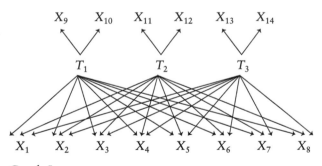

Graph 5

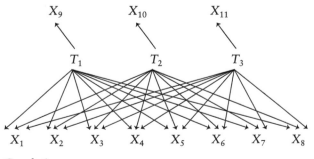

Graph 6

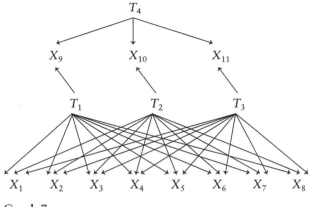

Graph 7

Each *e* is a distinct independently distributed variable, and each X variable has a distinct error term not shown in the graphs. I gave each of the exogenous variables, including the error terms, a mean of 0 and a variance of 1; I randomly assigned linear coefficients between 0.5 and 1.5, and generated the covariance matrices. The models, with a (required) phoney sample size of 32,000, were give to two programs: the default-principal-factors (4M) program in BMDP and the principal-components program in EQS. EQS has a default calculation of the number of factors; BMDP uses a constant in determining the number of factors and suggests that the constant be set equal to 1 divided by the number of measured variables, which was done. So far as I can tell, this rule for setting the constant is about optimal for these cases.

How do these programs do at determining the number of latent common factors in the structures that generated the covariances? The graphical representation brings to notice an ambiguity in the question. How do we count the number of latent common causes of a set of measured variables? Do we count the number of zero-indegree nonnoise ancestors of any two or more measured variables, or do we count the number of parents of any two or more measured variables? The rank theorem applies to the number of parents only. By the first count, zero-indegree ancestors, graph 1 has two common causes of the X variables; by the second count, parents, it has three. Table 14.1 reports the number of factors reported by the programs and the number of actual latents in the graphs, according to the two ways of counting.

Table 14.1
The number of latent factors identified by BMDP and EQS from simulated data

	Graph						
	1	2	3	4	5	6	7
No. of 0-indegree ancestors of measured variables	2	1	1	3	3	3	4
No. of parents of measured variables	3	3	3	3	3	3	4
BMDP no. of latents	1	1	3	2	*	3	3
EQS no. of latents	1	1	1	1	3	3	2

The asterisk (*) indicates a case for which BMDP would not converge.

The only generalization that seems true is that both programs report no more factors than there are parents of two or more measured variables. Only twice was BMDP right about the number of zero-indegree ancestors, and only twice was it right about the number of parents of two or more variables. EQS was right four times out of seven about the number of zero-indegree ancestors, and two times out of seven about the number of parents.

This example is only an illustration of the sort of thing that would have to be done far more extensively, and come out far better, to afford any evidence that, on the eight assumptions described earlier, factor analysis is reliable in various respects. (The BMDP program I used, for example, assumes that the latent variables are uncorrelated, and a procedure that allows "oblique rotation" might do better on the first three structures. But notice that the BMDP procedure did no better on the four structures in which the latent factors were uncorrelated than on the three structures in which the latents were correlated.) Although there are fragmentary simulation studies of special cases, so far as I can tell, studies of this sort are rarely done, never described in the documentation for commercial factor-analysis programs, and an adequate study of this kind—surveying a reasonable variety of structures, a variety of factor analysis procedures, and the sundry properties they are supposed to discover—has never been done at all. The only simulation tests I have found of the reliability of programs at finding the number of latent factors fail to make clear what that means, and assume besides that the factors are uncorrelated. The assumption seems unwarranted. If we adopt for the moment the first four basic psychometric assumptions, then on any of several pictures the distribution of unmeasured factors should be correlated. Suppose, for example, that the factors have genetic causes that vary from person to person; there is no reason to think the expression of genes for various factors are independently distributed. Suppose, again, that the factors are measures of the functioning or capacities of localized and physically linked modules. Then we should expect that how well one module works may depend on, and in turn influence, how well other modules linked to it work. Even so, a great number, perhaps the majority, of factor-analytic studies assume that the factors are uncorrelated; I cannot think of any reason for this assumption except, if wishes are sometimes reasons, the wish that it be so.

What credence should we give to the eight assumptions identified earlier? The eighth—that two or more latent factors must not perfectly cancel the effects of one another on measured responses—seems quite harmless and common to almost all good sciences; one can find its ancestor in Isaac Newton's Rules of Reasoning. The seventh—essentially, that there is no sample-selection bias—could be warranted by random sampling from the population, although I think that is rarely done. The sixth—normality and linearity—is harder to justify, but at least indirect evidence could be obtained from the marginal distributions of the measured variables and the appearance of constraints on the correlation matrix characteristic of linear dependencies, although tests for such constraints seem rarely to be done. In any case, the other issues could be repeated for nonlinear factor analysis. The fifth assumption—that all correlations are due to unmeasured common causes—is known to be false of various psychometric and sociometric instruments, in which the responses given to earlier questions influence the responses given to later questions. The fourth—that other features of persons influence their scores on psychometric tests—is uncontroversial. The third—that the function giving the dependence of manifest responses on hidden features is the same for all persons—is without any foundation, but if the dependencies were actually linear, independently varying coefficients for different persons would not change the constraints that factor models impose on large-sample correlation matrices. The best evidence for the second assumption—that the features of persons that produce their responses to psychometric test questions are fixed, constant, within each person—is the high test-retest correlations of IQ scores, but that argument meets a number of contrary considerations, for example, the dependence of scores on teachable fluency in the language in which the test is given.

There is another quite different consideration to which I give considerable weight. I have found very little speculation in the psychometric literature about the mechanisms by which unmeasured features or factors are thought to bring about measured responses, and none that connects psychometric factors with the decomposition of abilities that cognitive neuropsychology began to reveal at about the same time psychometrics was conceived. Neither Spearman nor later psychometricians, so far as I know, thought of the factors as modular capacities, localized in specific tissues, nor did they connect them with distributed aspects of specific brain functions. (It may be that Spearman thought of his latent *g* more the way we think of virtues of character than the way we think of causes.) One of the early psychometricians, Godfrey Thomson, thought of the brain as a more or less homogeneous neural net, and argued that different cognitive tasks require more or less neural activity according to their difficulty. Thomson thought this picture accounted not only for the correlations of test scores but also for the "hierarchies" of correlations that were the basis of Spearman's argument for "general intelligence." The picture, as well as other considerations, led Thomson to reject all the assumptions I have listed. I think a more compelling reason to reject them is the failure of psychometrics to produce predictive (rather than post-hoc) meshes with an ever more elaborate understanding of the components of normal capacities. Psychometrics did nothing to predict the varieties of dyslexias, aphasia, agnosias, and other cognitive ills that can result from brain damage.

Drawing conclusions about factor analysis is a dangerous business because the literature is too large for anyone with any other interest in life to survey. For all I know, asymptotic reliability proofs may exist, and excellent and thorough simulation studies may have been done, but I have not found much that addresses the central questions. To all appearances, astrology is better tested than factor analysis. With a very few exceptions, what I find instead are very modest simulation studies of special cases, statistical studies of the properties of estimators—studies that presuppose exactly what is in doubt, the credibility of factor models

—and introductory discussions that raise the issue of reliability only to evade it. There is some relevant theoretical work. Representing the most recent of a sequence of papers by several authors focused on when there exists a single common cause of observed measures, Junker and Ellis (1997) have provided necessary and sufficient conditions for the existence of a unidimensional latent-variable model of any real-valued measures. Spirtes et al. (1993, 2001) have shown that if the investigator provides a correct, initial division of variables into disjoint clusters such that the members of each cluster share at least a distinct latent common cause, then under certain assumptions, including linearity, unidimensional measurement models may be found for each latent, if it exists, and from such models and the data, some causal relations among latents may reliably be found.

Stephen Jay Gould (in Fraser 1995) claims that one of the essential premises of *The Bell Curve* is that there is a single common factor *g* responsible for performance on intelligence tests. No doubt Herrnstein and Murray make that assumption, but it is largely inessential to their argument. If IQ scores measured a pastiche of substantially heritable features that doom people to misery, the argument of *The Bell Curve* would be much the same. So the more important questions for assessing *The Bell Curve* concern causal relations between whatever it is IQ measures and various social outcomes. This brings us to regression, which, with its sibling, analysis of variance, plays a larger role than factor analysis in contemporary social statistics.

14.6   Regression and Discovery

Herrnstein and Murray begin the second part of their book (1994) with a description of some of their methods, and what the methods are used to do. I ask the reader to keep in mind their account from pages 72–75. I have numbered their paragraphs for subsequent reference:

(1)   The basic tool for multivariate analysis in the social sciences is known as regression analysis. The many forms of regression analysis have a common structure. There is a result to explain, the dependent variable. There are some things that might be the causes, the independent variables. Regression analysis tells how much each cause actually affects the result, taking the role of all the other hypothesized causes into account—an enormously useful thing for a statistical procedure to do, hence its widespread use.

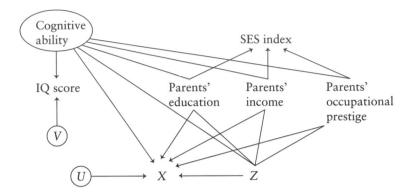

Figure 14.6
Note that undirected edges represent correlations whose causal mechanism is not specified.

(2)   In most of the chapters of Part II, we will be looking at a variety of social behaviors, ranging from crime to childbearing to unemployment to citizenship. In each instance, we will look first at the direct relationship of cognitive ability to that behavior. After observing a statistical connection, the next question to come to mind is, What else might be another source of the relationship?

(3)   In the case of IQ the obvious answer is socioeconomic status. . . . Our measure of SES is an index combining indicators of parental education, income, and occupational prestige. . . . Our basic procedure has been to run regression analyses in which the independent variables include IQ and parental SES. The result is a statement of the form "Here is the relationship of IQ to social behavior X after the effects of socioeconomic background have been extracted," or vice versa.

The causal picture Herrnstein and Murray seem to have in mind is that in figure 14.6, where the features in circles or ovals are unobserved, and the lines without arrows indicate statistical associations that may be due to influences in one direction or the other, or to unobserved common causes, or both. Z varies from case to case; often it is age.

If this were the correct causal story, then if very little of the variation in IQ scores between individuals were due to V, one could estimate the influence of cognitive ability on X (the behavior under consideration) by the two methods Herrnstein and Murray use: multiple regression of X on IQ and SES (socioeconomic status) index when the dependencies are all linear, and by logistic regression on those variables under other distribution assumptions. By "could estimate" I mean that the expected values of estimates of parameters would equal their true values.

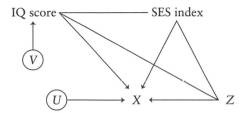

Figure 14.7

I will sometimes simplify the diagram in figure 14.6 as Herrnstein and Murray simplify their discussion (see figure 14.7). Under the assumptions just mentioned, if estimates of the influence of IQ score based on the causal model of figure 14.6 are correct, so are estimates of IQ based on the simpler surrogate structure of figure 14.7.

Now the standard objection to assuming something like the structure of figure 14.6 or figure 14.7 is put in terms of "correlated error." The objection is that in the corresponding regression equation, the error term U for X may be correlated with any of IQ, SES, and Z, that such correlation cannot be detected from the data, and that when it exists, the regression estimates of the influence of cognitive ability on X will be incorrect. Unless correlations arise by sheer chance, the correlation of U and IQ, say, will typically be due to some common causal pathway connecting IQ scores with whatever features are disguised by the variable U. A "correlated error" between a regressor such as IQ and the outcome variable X is typically the manifestation of some unknown cause or causes influencing both variables.[4]

Suppose that something else, denoted by W—mother's character, attention to small children, the number of siblings, the place in birth order, the presence of two parents, a scholarly tradition, a strong parental positive attitude towards learning, where (rather than how long) parents went to school, whatever—influences both cognitive ability and X. Then the regression estimates of the influence of cognitive ability on X based on the model in figure 14.6 will compound that influence with the association between cognitive ability and X produced by W (figure 14.8, or more briefly, figure 14.9). Here is how Herrnstein and Murray respond:

(4) We can already hear critics saying, "If only they had added this other variable to the analysis, they would have seen that intelligence has nothing to

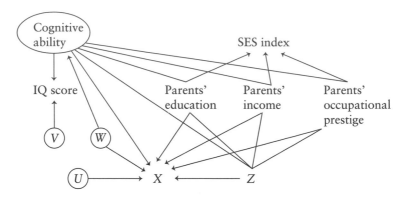

Figure 14.8

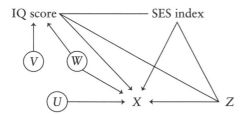

Figure 14.9

do with X." A major part of our analysis accordingly has been to anticipate what other variables might be invoked and seeing if they do in fact attenuate the relationship of IQ to any given social behavior.

This sounds quite sensible, until one notes that none of the possible confounding variables suggested above, nor many others that can easily be imagined, are considered in *The Bell Curve*, and until one reads the following:

(5)   At this point, however, statistical analysis can become a bottomless pit. . . . Our principle was to explore additional dynamics where there was another factor that was not only conceivably important but for clear logical reasons might be important because of dynamics having little or nothing to do with IQ. This last proviso is crucial, for one of the common misuses of regression analysis is to introduce an additional variable that in reality is mostly another expression of variables that are already in the equation.

There is a legitimate concern in this remark, which does not, however, excuse the neglect: if *W* is an *effect* of cognitive ability, then including *W* among the regressors will omit the mechanism that involves *W* and will

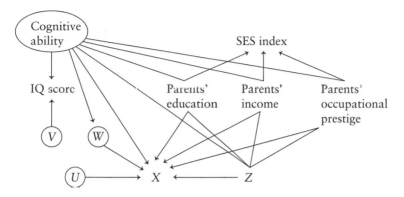

Figure 14.10

lead to an incorrect estimate of the overall influence of cognitive ability on *X* (figure 14.10).

Contrary to Herrnstein and Murray's remark in paragraph (5), however, it is exactly the presence of other variables that are common causes of *X* and of cognitive ability or IQ, and therefore "having to do" with cognitive ability or IQ, that lead to the "correlated errors" problem in estimating the influence of cognitive ability on *X*. Omitting such variables, if they exist, ensures that the regression estimates of effects are wrong. *The surprising fact is that the regression estimates may very well be wrong even if such variables are included in the regression.* That requires some explanation.

The authors of *The Bell Curve* have been criticized for omitting the subjects' educations from their set of regressors, an omission about which I will have more to say later. But their analysis would have been no better for including education. Suppose that the true causal structure is as in figure 14.10, with *W* representing years of education. Then multiple regression with education included would mistake the influence of cognitive ability on *X*, because it would leave out all pathways from cognitive ability to *X* that pass through *W*. At least, one might say, a regression that includes education would tell us how much cognitive ability influences *X other than* through mechanisms involving education, SES, and *Z*. But even that is not so. If there are additional unmeasured common causes of education and *X*, the error in the estimate of the separate effect of cognitive ability on *X* might be positive or negative. There are circumstances, arguably quite common circumstances, in which

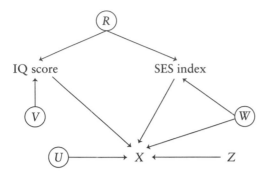

Figure 14.11

assumptions about distribution families (normal, etc.) are satisfied, and there is no "correlated error" between an outcome variable X and a regressor such as cognitive ability—that is, there is no unmeasured common cause of X and the regressor—but regression nonetheless mistakes the influence of the regressor on the outcome.

Suppose that the actual structure is as in figure 14.11. Notice that there is no unmeasured common cause of IQ and X, no correlation of the error term with IQ in the regression equation for X, but the error term in the regression equation is correlated with another regressor, SES. In this case, multiple regression of X on IQ, SES, and Z will give an incorrect estimate of the influence of IQ on X. The error of the estimate can be arbitrarily large and either positive or negative, depending on the values of the parameters associated with the unmeasured R and W variables. For all we know, the subjects in the data of Herrnstein and Murray's study are rich in such Rs and Ws.

Critics have noted that the SES index Herrnstein and Murray use is rather lame, but the criticism is largely beside the point. Suppose that they had used a better index, compounded of more measured features of the subjects and their families. The variables in SES indices may be strongly correlated, but they typically have no single common cause— those Herrnstein and Murray use demonstrably do not.[5] So a better index would add a lot of causally disparate measures together. Wouldn't that make it all the more likely that there are unmeasured variables, structurally like W in figure 14.10, influencing X and also influencing one or more of the components of SES? I think so.

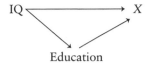

Figure 14.12

Adding extra variables to their study would not necessarily improve the accuracy of their estimates and might make them much worse, but leaving extra variables out may result in terribly inaccurate estimates.

Herrnstein and Murray remark that an obvious additional variable to control for is education, but they do not, first because years of education are caused by both SES and IQ, second because the effect of education on other variables is not linear and depends on whether certain milestones, graduations, have been passed, third because the correlation of education with SES and IQ makes for unstable estimates of regression coefficients, and fourth for the following reason:

(6) To take education's regression coefficient seriously tacitly assumes that education and intelligence could vary independently and produce similar results. No one can believe this to be true in general: indisputably giving nineteen years of education to a person with an IQ of 75 is not going to have the same impact on life as it would for a person with an IQ of 125.

(7) Our solution to this situation is to report the role of cognitive ability for two sub populations of the NLSY that each have the same level of education: a high school diploma, no more and no less in one group; a bachelor's degree, no more and no less, in the other. This is a simple, but we believe reasonable, way of bounding the degree to which cognitive ability makes a difference independent of education.

The third reason is unconvincing, since SES and IQ are already strongly correlated. The last reason, in paragraph (6), is unconvincing as a ground for omitting education from the analysis, but correct in supposing that there is an interaction. The interesting thing, however, is the alternative procedure suggested in paragraph (7), since it reveals a problem related to the problem of conditional correlated error that we have just discussed.

Herrnstein and Murray make it plain—they even draw the graph—that they have in mind a particular causal picture (see figure 14.12). If this is the correct structure, then if there is no interaction between IQ

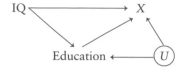

Figure 14.13

and education in their influence on *X*, one way to estimate the direct effect of IQ on *X* is to condition on any value of education. The point of measuring IQ and *X* for subjects with two values of education, I take it, is to give us some idea of how much the interaction makes this estimate unstable.

Here is the problem: What if figure 14.12 is *not* the correct causal structure? What if, instead, the correct causal structure is figure 14.13, whatever *U* may be. In that case, the association between IQ and *X* conditional on a value of education will not be a measure of the direct influence of IQ on *X*, and the error can be as large as you please, positive or negative, depending on *U* and the parameters associated with it.

This sort of problem, *sample selection bias,* can occur whenever membership in a sample is influenced by variables whose influence on one another is under investigation. It may happen, for example, when using a sample of hospitalized patients, or when using college students as subjects in psychological experiments, or when subjects in a longitudinal study are lost, or simply when using a subsample determined by values of a variable with complex causal relations, as Herrnstein and Murray do. The same error can be found in other works in social psychology, for example, in Helgeson et al. 1999.

14.7   The Problems of Causal Inference

Herrnstein and Murray use the tools that their professions, and social statistics generally, gave to them. The tools are incompetent for the use Herrnstein and Murray put them to, but what else were they to do? What else can anyone do who is trying to understand the causal structure at work in processes that cannot be controlled experimentally?

Consider for a moment some of the difficulties in the problem of trying to infer causation from observed correlations:

1. Little may actually be known beforehand about the causal relations, or absence of causal relations, among variables. In typical social studies, time order often provides the only reliable information—negative information, at that—about cause and effect.

2. Observed associations may be due to unmeasured or unrecorded common causes.

3. There may be a vast number of alternative possible hypotheses—the larger the number of measured variables, the more astronomical the set of possible causal structures. When latent variables are allowed, the number of possible causal structures is literally infinite.

4. Several or even a great many hypothetical structures may equally account for the same correlations, no matter how large the sample, and in finite samples a great many models may fit the data quite well.

5. The sample may be unrepresentative of a larger population because membership in the sample is influenced by some of the very features whose causal relations are the object of study.

6. The sample may be unrepresentative by chance.

7. Values for sundry variables may be unrecorded for some units in the sample.

8. The joint distribution of variables may not be well approximated by any of the familiar distributions of statistics. In particular, there may be combinations of continuous variables and variables that take only a finite set of values.

9. Relations among variables may be complicated by feedback, as between education and IQ.

Many of the same difficulties beset causal inference in experimental contexts, even though experimental design aims to remove the possibility of confounding common causes of treatment and to maximize prior knowledge of the causal structure of the experimental system. Psychological experiments often concern unobserved and uncontrolled features; clinical experiments sometimes try to investigate multiple treatments and multiple outcomes simultaneously, with entirely parallel problems about confounding and feedback, especially in longitudinal studies. Sample selection and attrition in experiments, especially experiments with humans, can create selection bias as in (5) and can result in missing values. The distribution of treatments in experiments is controlled by the experimenter, but the distribution of outcomes, which may conform to no familiar pattern, is not. And subjects may not conform to an experimental regimen.

We can imagine a black box that addresses these problems. Data and relevant beliefs are put in, causal information comes out, and inside the box the problems just listed are taken account of. The box is imaginary, of course. There are no methods available that more or less automatically address all of these problems. There is no computer program that will take the data and prior knowledge, automatically take account of missing values, distributions, possible selection bias, possible feedback, possible latent variables, and reliably and informatively give back the possible causal explanations that produce good approximations to the data, information about error bounds, or posterior probabilities. But we can think of the box as an ideal, not only for inference but also for forcing practitioners to cleanly separate the claims they make before examining the data from the claims they believe are warranted by the data. How close do the methods used by Herrnstein and Murray and other social scientists come to the ideal box? And how close could they come were they to use available, if nonstandard, methods?

Let us leave aside some of these problems and suppose that our samples are good and distributed nicely (normally, say), that there are no missing values, no feedback, and no sample selection bias. Consider for a moment in this context using regression to decide a simpler question than estimating the influence of cognitive ability on X from ideal data on X, cognitive ability, and a definite set of other regressors: does cognitive ability have any influence *at all* on X? Multiple regression will lead to a negative answer when the partial regression coefficient for cognitive ability is not significantly different from zero. Under a normal distribution, this is essentially an assumption connecting the absence of causal influence with a conditional-independence fact, namely that *cognitive ability does not (directly) influence X if and only if cognitive ability and X are independent conditional on the set of all of the other regressors.*

We have observed in the previous section that the principle in the italicized phrase is false, in fact intensely false. Indeed, without a priori causal knowledge, there is no way to get reliable causal information of any sort from multiple regression. If one should be so fortunate as to know independently of the data analysis that there are no common causes of any of the regressors and the outcome variable and that the outcome variable is not a cause of any of the regressors, then under appropriate distribution assumptions, regression gives the right answer. Otherwise not.

Regression does a funny thing: to evaluate the influence of one regressor on X, it conditions on *all other* regressors, but not on any proper subsets of other regressors. Stepwise regression procedures typically do investigate the dependence of a regressor and X conditional on various subsets of other regressors, but they do so in completely ad hoc ways, with no demonstrable connection between the procedures and getting to the truth about causal structure. Regression and stepwise regression reflect intuitions from experimental design and elsewhere that absence of causation has something to do with conditional independence. They simply don't get the something right. The correct relationship is far more complicated.

Fifteen years ago Terry Speed and his student Harry Kiiveri (Kiiveri and Speed 1982) introduced a correct relation, which, with some historical inaccuracy, they called a Markov condition. Speed has since testified to the correctness of the principle in the most infamous trial of our time. The Markov Assumption was discussed in detail in chapter 3, but I will rehearse it once more for readers who came in late. Understanding the condition requires that one variable, Y, say, is a *direct cause* of another, X, relative to a set of variables D to which X and Y both belong. Y is a direct cause of X relative to D if there is a causal pathway from Y to X that does not contain any other variable in D—in other words, there is no set of variables in D such that if we were to intervene to fix values for variables in that set, variations in Y would no longer influence X. We need one further preliminary definition: I will say that any set D of variables is *causally sufficient*, provided that every direct common cause of two variables in D is in D.

Causal Markov Assumption For any variable X and any set of variables Z that are not effects of X (and that do not include X as a member) and any causally sufficient set D of variables including Z and having X as a member, X is independent of Z conditional on the set of members of D that are direct causes of X—the set of parents of X in the directed graph of causal relations.

When true, the Markov condition gives a sufficient causal condition for conditional independence. The converse condition gives necessity:

Faithfulness Condition   All conditional independencies in a causal system result from the Causal Markov condition.

The scope of the Markov condition is occasionally misunderstood by philosophical commentators, and a result from chapters 3 and 5 bears repeating:

Need for Markov Assumption   As a formal principle about directed graphs and probability distributions, the Markov Assumption is necessary if exogenous variables (including errors or noises) are independent and each variable is a deterministic function of its parents (including among parents, any errors or noises). The form of the functional dependence is irrelevant.

In a system whose causal structure is represented by a direct acyclic graph and that generates a probability distribution meeting the Markov Assumption for that graph, the faithfulness assumption will fail if two variables are connected by two or more causal pathways (either from one variable to another or from a third variable to both) that exactly cancel one another, or if some of the relations among variables (excluding error terms) are deterministic. In practice, both the Markov and faithfulness assumptions are consistent with almost every causal model in the social-scientific literature, nonlinear models included, that does not purport to represent feedback or reciprocal influence.

We can use these two conditions to discover what the conditional independencies implied by the structures that Herrnstein and Murray postulate could *possibly* tell us, by any method whatsoever, about those structures. That is, we will suppose that their causal story is correct and ask whether they could reasonably infer it is correct from data that nicely agrees with it. To do so, we need some simple representations of ignorance about causal structures. Here is a convenient code:

$X \circ\!\!-\!\!\circ Y$ X is a cause of Y, or Y is a cause of Y, or there is a common unmeasured cause of X and of Y, or one of X, Y causes the other and there is also an unmeasured common cause.

$X \circ\!\!-\!\!\rightarrow Y$ X is a cause of Y, or there is a common unmeasured cause of X and of Y, or both.

$X \longleftrightarrow Y$ There is a common unmeasured cause of X and of Y, but neither X nor Y influences the other.

With these conventions, here is what the conditional independencies implied by the causal hypothesis of figure 14.7 tell us about causal rela-

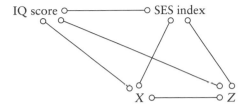

Figure 14.14

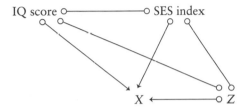

Figure 14.15

tions: *nothing at all* about whether IQ score is a cause of X (figure 14.14).

Suppose that common sense tells us that X is not a cause of the other variables. That doesn't help much. The result is figure 14.15. We still can't tell whether IQ has any influence at all on X. For all we know from the conditional independencies in the data and prior knowledge, the association between IQ scores and X is produced entirely by the variation of unmeasured factors that influence both IQ score and X. The sizes and signs of the observed covariances in this case would give no other extra information about the actual causal structure.

The Markov and faithfulness assumptions also entail that there are possible causal relations that we can determine from observed associations, provided we have none of the problems (5) through (9) listed above. For example, suppose that we have measures of A, B, C and D, and that their causal relations are actually as in figure 14.16. Then according to the two assumptions, we can determine from independence facts the causal structure in figure 14.17, and so that C is actually a cause of D. Moreover, there is a certain robustness to the determination, for if we were to decide that the independencies corresponding to figure 14.16 obtain when in fact they do not quite because of a small common cause of C and D, and if the association of A and C or B and C is large,

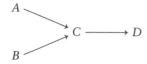

Figure 14.16

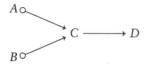

Figure 14.17

then (in the linear case, at any rate) the estimate of the influence of C on D obtained using the result in figure 14.17 will be a good approximation to the truth. There is here a general moral—almost never observed—about the kind of data one should seek if causal relations are to be inferred from observed data.

The Markov and faithfulness assumptions can just as well give us information about the presence of unmeasured common causes. Consider the imaginary causal structure in figure 14.18. The Markov and faithfulness conditions imply that the independence and conditional-independence relations associated with the structure in figure 14.18 uniquely determine the information in figure 14.19—figure 14.19 is what can be determined in principle from data using the correlations and partial correlations.

These remarks would be of little practical use if in any application one were required to prove some intricate theorem, distinct for almost every case, characterizing the structures consistent with prior knowledge and the patterns of independence and conditional independence found in the data. No such effort is necessary. There are general algorithms,[7] freely available in the TETRAD III program, that do the computations for any case. The procedures are rarely used, certainly not by Herrnstein and Murray or their critics. Were they used, social scientists would at least be forced to be entirely explicit about the causal assumptions that they have forced on their data analysis.

In keeping with social-scientific tradition, Herrnstein and Murray give endless pages of statistical conclusions, but their data are all but hidden;

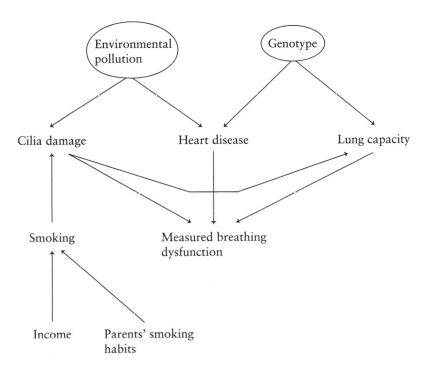

Figure 14.18

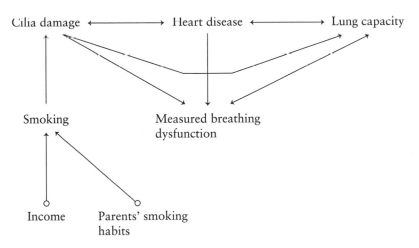

Figure 14.19

one has to go to the original sources and know the sample they selected from it. Although Herrnstein and Murray report any number of linear regressions with results determined entirely by a simple covariance matrix, they give only one such matrix in the entire book, and no count data. Even so, we have excellent reason to think that scientific searches applied to the data they use would turn up structures such as those in figure 14.18, structures permitting no causal inferences of the kind Murray and Herrnstein wish to draw.

14.8   Projects and Attitudes

There may never be an inference box that addresses all of the problems of causal inference from observational data, but there can certainly be boxes that can help social and behavioral scientists do better than they will do armed only with their preconceptions, factor analysis, and regression. The more model specification is automated and data-driven and the more substantive prior assumptions are mechanically separated from inferences made from the data, the more algorithms in the box give out only information justified by explicit assumptions and the less likely is the kind of work *The Bell Curve* represents.

Notes

Chapter 2

1. As Susan Sterrett kindly pointed out to me, along with the differences in Turing's imitation games.

2. A Madelyn Rose joke: What two Presidents were named Rose? (Answer: Teddy and Franklin.)

3. Madelyn's explanation: Venus moves faster than Earth, which moves faster than Mars. Why? Because Venus is closer to the Sun than Earth, and Earth is closer than Mars. Planets closer to the Sun are hotter than planets farther from the Sun. Hotter things move faster than cold things.

4. See Kelly, *The Logic of Reliable Inquiry* (1996).

5. I do not mean to suggest that only Gopnik and Meltzoff present them. Related ideas may be found, for example, in works by Susan Carey, Henry Wellman, Annette Karmilov-Smith, and others, but I think they are nowhere put so forcefully or generally as in Gopnik and Meltzoff's book (1997).

6. There is a nice historical circle to the theory theory. Both Thomas Kuhn and Jean Piaget have obviously influenced Gopnik and Meltzoff. In the preface to *The Structure of Scientific Revolutions*, Kuhn cites Piaget (and *The Child's Conception of Causality*, in particular) as one of his sources of inspiration, and some of his most famous terminology is derived from Piaget. Now the theory theorists want to take Kuhn's philosophy of science back to development, but closer to Enlightenment conceptions of rationality.

7. This is equivalent in many contexts to a standard Bayesian criterion of reliable convergence to the truth, and is the criterion used in many mathematical studies of language learning.

8. For details and references, see Kelly, *The Logic of Reliable Inquiry* (1996).

9. See Kelly, *The Logic of Reliable Inquiry* (1996). Reliability analysis in learning theory with conceptual changes seems a formal solution to the problem of giving a rational account of scientific progress consistent with Kuhn's conceptual relativism. Kuhn spent his years after the publication of *The Structure of Scientific Revolutions* (1970) searching, in vain, for such a solution.

Chapter 3

1. The alert reader will have noted that, in the toy train example, if both the engine and the caboose are separately pulled, there is no directed, acyclic graphical representation of the causal relations.

2. Randomizing treatments in a sample does not remove the influence of other factors on any particular member of the sample. Rather, it reduces the chance that other factors produce an average difference between treated and control subsamples.

3. If x influences y through two or more distinct mechanisms, the influences may cancel, which would make x and y independent but causally connected.

4. The remark requires technical qualification in view of unpublished work by Jamie Robins, Richard Scheines, Peter Spirtes, and Larry Wasserman. If a set of variables is causally sufficient and a time order is known, there are search procedures that uniformly converge to the true structure as the sample size increases without bound—meaning that one could construct a kind of confidence interval for the estimated structure. Absent those assumptions, the procedures can only converge nonuniformly—meaning that eventually any particular alternative to the truth can be rendered arbitrarily improbable, but there will always exist, for any finite sample, alternatives that are not improbable. See chapter 12 of Spirtes et al. 2000 for details.

Chapter 7

1. Equation (1) has a long history. The first occurrence I know of is in a paper in the 1850s by the great nineteenth-century mathematician Arthur Cayley, responding to a problem about causal inference posed by George Boole. Cayley assumes that U and C are independent. Boole objected to Cayley's solution to his problem, but the solution, and equation (3), were defended by Richard Dedekind. Cayley's argument for (3) was quite different from Cheng's. (For a discussion, references, and the relevant passages from Cayley, Dedekind, and Boole, see Hailperin 1986.) Equation (9) was introduced in epidemiology in the middle of the last century (Sheps 1958).

Chapter 9

1. This chapter was motivated by enlightening discussions with Alison Gopnik and Joshua Tenenbaum. The analysis presented here developed from subsequent discussions with Peter Spirtes.

Chapter 10

1. I believe that Jerry Fodor's *The Modularity of Mind* misread the history as about "modules" that are "informationally encapsulated"—that is, the func-

tioning of modules is unaffected by "beliefs." Part of Fodor's motivation for this vague condition seems to have been to provide a psychological basis for refuting Kuhnian perceptual relativism, but I think it has no real basis in current or historical neuropsychological practice. About beliefs and cognitive parts, there seem to me only two alternatives: either the property of having a belief that p counts across physical realizations, and so states of cognitive parts, and hence cannot be an influence on the state of a cognitive part, or else whatever physics corresponds to beliefs could very well be input to a cognitive part and influence its response to other inputs. Neuropsychologists who have adopted Fodor's terminology misdescribe their own practice.

Chapter 11

1. Neuropsychology has generally made comparatively little use of response times, and I will ignore them here. But see the excellent study by Luce (1986) for a discussion of response-time problems related to those considered in this chapter.

Chapter 13

1. For examples, see McClelland and Rumelhart 1986; Cohen and Servan-Schreiber 1989; Levine 1986; Bapi and Levine 1990; Levine and Prucitt 1989; Carpenter and Grossberg 1987; Cohen et al., in press; Hinton and Shallice 1991; Mozer and Behrmann 1990; Patterson et al. 1990.

2. This chapter is joint work with Thomas Richardson and Peter Spirtes.

Chapter 14

1. Beginning with Spearman (1904) and ending (so far as I know) with Jones and Spearman (1950).

2. C. Glymour (1980) gives an account of Dalton's simplicity principle and its empirical difficulties.

3. There is an open technical issue here. There are cases in which a covariance matrix generated by a model with correlated error cannot be reproduced by that model but with each correlated error replaced by a distinct latent variable and the latent variables are uncorrelated—the question is whether such matrices can always be reproduced from an appropriate latent-variable structure.

4. Herrnstein and Murray give a correlation matrix for their four SES variables. The TETRAD II program (Scheines 1994) will automatically test for vanishing tetrad differences not implied by vanishing partial correlations in the matrix. If there is a single common cause, there should be three such differences. There are none.

5. The example is due to Chris Meek.

6. Given in Spirtes et al. 1993, 2000.

7. The covariance matrix is given in Spirtes et al. 1993, 2000.

References

Allan, L. (1980). "A Note on Measurement of Contingency between Two Binary Variables in Judgement Tasks." *Bulletin of the Psychonomic Society* 15: 147–149.

Baker, A. G., P. Mercier, F. Vallée-Tourangeau, R. Frank, and Maria Pan (1993). "Selective Associations and Causality Judgements: Presence of a Strong Causal Factor May Reduce Judgements of a Weaker One." *Journal of Experimental Psychology: Learning Memory and Cognition* 19: 414–432.

Bapi, R., and D. Levine (1990). "Networks Modeling the Involvement of the Frontal Lobes in Learning and Performance of Flexible Movement Sequences." In *Proceedings of the Twelfth Annual Conference of the Cognitive Science Society*, pp. 915–922.

Bates, E., J. McDonald, B. MacWhinney, and M. Appelbaum (1991). "A Maximum Likelihood Procedure for the Analysis of Group and Individual Data in Aphasia Research." *Brain and Language* 40: 231–265.

Beinlich, I. A., H. J. Suermondt, R. M. Chavez, and G. F. Cooper (1989). "The ALARM Monitoring System: A Case Study with Two Probabilistic Inference Techniques for Belief Networks." In *Proceedings of the Conference on Artificial Intelligence in Medical Care, London.*

Blau, Peter M., and Otis Dudley Duncan (1967). *The American Occupational Structure.* New York: Wiley.

Bouteliee, C., and M. Goldzmidt (1996). "The Frame Problem and Bayesian Network Action Representations." In *Proceedings of the Canadian Conference on Artificial Intelligence.*

Bub, J. (1994). "Testing Models of Cognition through the Analysis of Brain Damaged Performance." *British Journal for Philosophy of Science* 45: 837–855.

Bub, J., and D. Bub (1988). "On the Methodology of Single-Case Studies in Cognitive Neuropsychology." *Cognitive Neuropsychology* 5: 565–582.

Bub, J., and D. Bub (1991). "On Testing Models of Cognition Through the Analysis of Brain-Damaged Performance." Preprint.

Caramazza, A. (1984). "The Logic of Neuropsychological Research and the Problem of Patient Classification in Aphasia." *Brain and Language* 21: 9–20.

Caramazza, A. (1986). "On Drawing Inferences about the Structure of Normal Cognitive Systems from the Analysis of Patterns of Impaired Performance: The Case for Single-Patient Studies." *Brain and Cognition* 5: 41–66.

Caramazza, A., and W. Badecker (1989). "Patient Classification in Neuropsychological Research." *Brain and Cognition* 16: 256–295.

Caramazza, A., and M. McCloskey (1988). "The Case for Single-Patient Studies." *Cognitive Neuropsychology* 5: 517–527.

Carnap, Rudolf (1967). *The Logical Structure of the World.* Berkeley: University of California Press.

Carpenter, G., and S. Grossberg (1987). "A Massively Parallel Architecture for a Self-Organizing Neural Pattern Recognition Machine." *Computer Vision, Graphics, and Image Processing* 37: 54–115.

Cartwright, Nancy (1989). *Nature's Capacities and Their Measurement.* New York: Oxford University Press.

Cheng, Patricia (1997). "From Covariation to Causation: A Causal Power Theory." *Psychological Review* 104: 367–405.

Cheng, Patricia (1999). "Causality in the Mind: Estimating Contextual and Conjunctive Power." In F. Keil and R. Wilson, eds., *Explanation and Cognition.* Cambridge: MIT Press.

Cheng, Patricia, and Laura Novick (1990). "A Probabilistic Contrast Model of Causal Induction." *Journal of Personality and Social Psychology* 58: 545–557.

Cheng, Patricia, and Laura Novick (1999). "Assessing Interactive Causal Influence." Preprint, Department of Psychology, UCLA.

Cohen, J., and D. Servan-Schreiber (1989). "A Parallel Distributed Processing Approach to Behavior and Biology in Schizophrenia." Technical Report AIP-100, Department of Psychology, Carnegie Mellon University.

Cohen, J., R. Romero, and M. Farah (in press). "Disengaging from the Disengage Mechanism: A Re-interpretation of Attentional Deficits Following Parietal Damage." In *Proceedings of the Twentieth Annual Meeting of the International Neuropsychological Society.*

Cooper, G. F. (1990). "The Computational Complexity of Probabilistic Inference Using Bayesian Belief Networks." *Artificial Intelligence* 42: 393–405.

Cooper, G. F. (1999). "An Overview of the Representation and Discovery of Causal Relationships Using Bayesian Networks." In C. Glymour and G. F. Cooper, eds., *Computation, Causation, and Discovery.* Cambridge: MIT Press.

Cooper, G. F., and E. H. Herskovits (1992). "A Bayesian Method for the Induction of Probabilistic Networks from Data." *Machine Learning* 9: 309–347.

Cooper, G. F., and C. Yoo (1999). "Causal Discovery from a Mixture of Experimental and Observational Data." In *Proceedings of the Conference on Uncertainty in Artificial Intelligence,* pp. 116–125.

Danks, D. (2001). "The Epistemology of Causal Judgement." Ph.D thesis, Department of Philosophy, University of California, San Diego.

Dawes, R. (1988). "Rational Choice in an Uncertain World." San Diego: Harcourt Brace Jovanovich.

Druzdzel, Marek J., and C. Glymour (1994). "Application of the TETRAD 11 Program to the Study of Student Retention in U.S. Colleges." In *Working Notes of the AAAI-94 Workshop on Knowledge Discovery in Databases (KDD-94)*, pp. 419–430. Seattle, Wash.

Dunn, J. Michael (1990). "The Frame Problem and Relevant Predication." In H. Kyburg Jr., R. Loui, and G. Carlson, eds., *Knowledge Representation and Defeasible Reasoning*, pp. 89–95. New York: Kluwer.

Ellis, A., and A. Young (1988). *Human Cognitive Neuropsychology*. Hillsdale, N.J.: Lawrence Erlbaum.

Farah, Martha J. (1990). *Visual Agnosia*. Oxford: Oxford University Press.

Farah, Martha J. (1994). "Neuropsychological Inference with an Interactive Brain: A Critique of the 'Locality Assumption'." *Behavioral and Brain Sciences* 17: 43–61.

Fisher, Ronald A. (1958). *The Genetical Theory of Natural Selection*. New York: Dover.

Fodor, J. (1983). *Modularity of Mind: An Essay on Faculty Psychology*. Cambridge: MIT Press.

Fodor, J. (1987). "Modules, Frames, Frigeons, Sleeping Dogs and the Music of the Spheres." In Z. Pylyshyn, ed., *The Robot's Dilemma*, pp. 139–149. Norwood, N.J.: Ablex.

Fraser, Steven, ed. (1995). *The Bell Curve Wars*. New York: Basic Books.

Freud, Sigmund (1891). *On Aphasia*. Translated by E. Stengel. New York: International Universities Press, 1953.

Freud, Sigmund (1895). "Project for a Scientific Psychology." Translated in J. Strachey, ed., *The Complete Psychological Works of Sigmund Freud*. London: Macmillian.

Geiger, D., D. Heckerman, and C. Meek (1996). "Asymptotic Model Selection for Directed Networks with Hidden Variables." Preprint, Microsoft Research Center.

Glymour, Clark (1980). *Theory and Evidence*. Princeton: Princeton University Press.

Glymour, Clark (1994). "On the Methods of Cognitive Neuropsychology." *British Journal for Philosophy of Science* 45: 815–835.

Glymour, Clark (1998). "Psychological and Normative Theories of Causal Power and the Probabilities of Causes." In G. Cooper and S. Moral, eds., *Uncertainty in Artificial Intelligence*, pp. 166–172. San Francisco: Morgan Kaufmann.

Glymour, Clark, and Gregory Cooper, eds. (1999). *Computation, Causation and Discovery*. Cambridge: MIT Press.

Glymour, Clark, Richard Scheines, Peter Spirtes, and Kevin Kelly (1987). *Discovering Causal Structure: Artificial Intelligence, Philosophy of Science, and Statistical Modeling*. Orlando: Academic Press.

Gold, E. Mark (1965). "Limiting Recursion." *Journal of Symbolic Logic* 30: 28–48.

Goodman, Nelson (1951). *The Structure of Appearance*. Cambridge: Harvard University Press.

Gopnik, A., and C. Glymour (in press). "Causal Maps and Bayes Nets: A Cognitive and Computational Account of Theory-Formation." In P. Carruthers, S. Stich, and M. Siegal, eds., *The Cognitive Basis of Science*. Cambridge: Cambridge University Press.

Gopnik, A., and A. Meltzoff (1997). *Words, Thoughts, and Theories*. Cambridge: MIT Press.

Gopnik, A., and T. Nazzi (in press). "Words, Kinds, and Causal Powers: A Theory Theory Perspective on Early Naming and Categorization." In D. Rakison and L. Oakes, eds., *Early Categorization*. Oxford: Oxford University Press.

Gopnik, A., and D. Sobel (2000). "Detecting Blickets: How Young Children Use Information about Novel Causal Powers in Categorization and Induction." Child Development 71, no. 5: 1205–1222.

Gopnik, A., D. Sobel, L. Schultz, and C. Glymour (in press). "Causal Learning Mechanisms in Very Young Children: Two, Three, and Four-Year-Old Infer Causal Relations from Patterns of Variation and Covariation." *Developmental Psychology*.

Gould, S. J. (1981). *The Mismeasure of Man*. New York: Norton.

Hailperin, Theodore (1986). *Boole's Logic and Probability*. New York: North-Holland.

Hashem, A. I., and G. F. Cooper (1996). "Human Causal Discovery from Observational Data." In *Proceedings of the Fall Symposium of the American Medical Informatics Association*, pp. 27–31.

Hayduk, L. (1996). *LISREL Issues, Debates, and Strategies*. Baltimore: Johns Hopkins Press.

Heckerman, D. (1995). "A Bayesian Approach to Learning Causal Networks." Technical report MSR-TR-95–04, Microsoft Research Center. http://www.research.microsoft.com/research/dtg/heckerma/heckerma.html.

Helgeson, V., S. Cohen, R. Schulz, and J. Yasko (1999). "Education and Peer Discussion Group Interventions and Adjustment to Breast Cancer." *Archives of General Psychiatry* 56: 340–347.

Herrnstein, Richard J., and Charles Murray (1994). *The Bell Curve: Intelligence and Class Structure in American Life*. New York: Free Press.

Hinton, G., and T. Shallice (1991). "Lesioning an Attractor Network: Investigations of Acquired Dyslexia." *Psychological Review* 98: 74–95.

Holland, Paul (1986). "Statistics and Causal Inference." *Journal of the American Statistical Association* 81: 945–960.

Johnson, Susan (2000). "The Recognition of Mentalistic Agents in Infancy." *Trends in Cognitive Sciences* 4, in press.

Jones, L. Wynn, and Charles Spearman (1950). *Human Ability: A Continuation of "The Abilities of Man."* London: Macmillan.

Jordan, M., ed. (1998). *Learning in Graphical Models.* Cambridge: MIT Press.

Joreskog, Karl, and Dag Sorbom (1990). "Model Search with Tetrad II and LISREL." *Sociological Methods and Research* 19: 93–106.

Juhl, C. (1997). "Objectively Reliable Subjective Probabilities." *Synthese* 109: 293–309.

Junker, B., and Jules L. Ellis (1997). "A Characterization of Monotone Unidimensional Latent Variable Models." *Annals of Statistics* 25: 1327–1343.

Kelly, Kevin (1996). *The Logic of Reliable Inquiry.* New York: Oxford University Press.

Kelly, Kevin, and O. Schulte (1995). "The Computable Testability of Theories Making Uncomputable Predictions." *Erkenntnis* 43: 29–66.

Kiiveri, Harry, and Terry Speed (1982). "Structural Analysis of Multivariate Data: A Review." In Samuel Leinhardt, ed., *Sociological Methodology.* San Francisco: Jossey-Boss.

Klahr, Danid, Pat Langley, and Robert Neches (1987). *Production System Models of Learning and Development.* Cambridge: MIT Press.

Kohn, Melvin L. (1967). *Class and Conformity: A Study of Values.* Homewood, Ill.: Dorsey Press.

Kosslyn, S., and J. Intriligator (1992). "Is Cognitive Neuropsychology Plausible? The Perils of Sitting on a One-Legged Stool." *Journal of Cognitive Neuroscience* 4: 96–107.

Kuhn, T. (1970). *The Structure of Scientific Revolutions.* Chicago: University of Chicago Press.

Kushnir, T. (2001). "Action at a Distance: How Spatial Contiguity Affects Preschool Children's Causal Understanding." Poster, Society for Research in Child Development.

Levine, D. (1986). "A Neural Network Theory of Frontal Lobe Function." In *Proceedings of the Eighth Annual Conference of the Cognitive Science Society*, pp. 716–727.

Levine, D., and P. Prueitt (1989). "Modeling Some Effects of Frontal Lobe Damage—Novelty and Perseveration." *Neural Networks* 2: 103–116.

Lewis, C. I. (1959). *Mind and the World Order.* New York: Dover.

Lien, Y., and Patricia Cheng (in press). "Distinguishing Genuine from Spurious Causes: A Coherence Hypothesis." *Cognitive Psychology.*

Lissauer, H. (1890). "Ein Fall von Seelenblindheit nebst einem Beitrag zur Theorie derselben." *Archiv für Psychiatrie* 21: 222–270.

Luce, R. D. (1986). *Response Times.* New York: Oxford University Press.

Madigan, D., A. E. Raftery, C. T. Volinsky, and J. A. Hoeting (1996). "Bayesian Model Averaging." *AAAI Workshop on Integrating Multiple Learned Models.* http://bayes.stat.washington.edu/papers.html.

Massaro, D. (1988). "Some Criticisms of Connectionist Models of Human Performance." *Journal of Memory and Language* 27: 213–234.

McCarthy, J., and P. Hayes (1969). "Some Philosophical Problems from the Standpoint of Artificial Intelligence." In D. Michie, ed., *Machine Intelligence*, pp. 463–502. New York: Elsevier.

McClelland, J., and D. Rumelhart (1986). "Amnesia and Distributed Memory." In J. McClelland, D. Rumelhart, and the PDP research group, eds., *Parallel Distributed Processing*, vol. 2. Cambridge: MIT Press.

McCloskey, M., and A. Caramazza (1988). "Theory and Methodology in Cognitive Neuropsychology: A Response to Our Critics." *Cognitive Neuropsychology* 5: 583–623.

McDermott, D. (1987). "We've Been Framed, or Why AI Is Innocent of the Frame Problem." In Z. Pylyshyn, ed., *The Robot's Dilemma*, pp. 113–122. New York: Ablex.

Melz, E., and P. Cheng, K. Holyoak, and M. Waldmann (1993). "Cue Competition in Huan Categorization: Contingency or the Rescorla-Wagner Learning Rule? Comment on Shanks (1991)." *Journal of Experimental Psychology, Learning Memory, and Cognition* 19: 1398–1410.

Mosteller, F., and J. W. Tukey (1977). *Data Analysis and Regression*. Reading, Mass.: Addison-Wesley.

Mozer, M., and M. Behrmann (1990). "On the Interaction of Selective Attention and Lexical Knowledge: A Connectionist Account of Neglect Dyslexia." *Journal of Cognitive Neuroscience* 2: 96–123.

Murray, Charles (1984). *Losing Ground: American Social Policy 1950–1980*. New York: Basic Books.

Nazzi, T., and A. Gopnik (2000). "A Shift in Children's Use of Perceptual and Causal Cues to Categorization." *Developmental Science* 3: 389–396.

Osherson, D., M. Stob, and S. Weinstein (1985). *Systems That Learn*. Cambridge: MIT Press.

Osherson, D., M. Stob, and S. Weinstein (1988). "Mechanical Learners Pay a Price for Bayesianism." *Journal of Symbolic Logic* 53 (4): 1245–1251.

Osherson, D., and S. Weinstein (1989). "Paradigms of Truth Detection." *Journal of Philosophical Logic* 18: 1–42.

Patterson, K., M. Seidenberg, and J. McClelland (1990). "Connections and Disconnections: Acquired Dyslexia in a Computational Model of Reading Processes." In R. Morris, ed., *Parallel Distributed Processing*. Oxford: Oxford University Press.

Pearl, Judea (1988). *Probabilistic Reasoning in Intelligent Systems: Networks of Plausible Inference*. San Mateo: Morgan Kaufman.

Pearl, Judea (1999). "Graphs, Structural Models and Causality." In C. Glymour and G. Cooper, eds., *Computation, Causation, and Discovery*. Cambridge: MIT Press.

Pearl, Judea (2000). *Causality*. Oxford: Oxford University Press.

Pearl, Judea, and R. Dechter (1996). "Identifying Independencies in Causal Graphs with Feedback." Technical report R-243, Cognitive Science Laboratory, UCLA.

Pearl, Judea, and T. Verma (1991). "A Theory of Inferred Causation." In *Principles of Knowledge Representation and Reasoning: Proceedings of the Second International Conference*. San Mateo, Calif.: Morgan Kaufmann.

Pearson, K. (1911). *The Grammar of Science*. London: A. and C. Black.

Piaget, J. (1930). *The Child's Conception of Physical Causality*. New York: Harcourt Brace.

Rehder, B. (1999). "A Causal Model Theory of Categorization." In *Proceedings of the 21st Annual Conference of the Cognitive Science Society*, pp. 595–600. Vancouver, B.C.

Rescorla, R. A., and A. R. Wagner (1972). "A Theory of Pavlovian Conditioning: Variations in the Effectiveness of Reinforcement and Nonreinforcement." In A. H. Black and W. F. Prokasy, eds., *Classical Conditioning II: Current Theory and Research*, pp. 64–99. New York: Appleton-Century-Crofts.

Richardson, T. (1994). "Properties of Cyclic Graphical Models." M.S. thesis, Carnegie Mellon University.

Richardson, T. (1996). "Discovering Cyclic Causal Structure." Technical report CMU Phil 68, Department of Philosophy, Carnegie Mellon University.

Russell, Bertrand (1956). *Our Knowledge of the External World*. London: G. Allen and Unwin.

Scheines, R. (1994). "Inferring Causal Structure among Unmeasured Variables." In *Proceedings of the Fourth International Workshop on Statistics and AI*. Ft. Lauderdale, Fla.: Springer-Verlag.

Scheines, R., and Anne Boomsma (1999). "Bayesian Estimation and Testing of Structural Equation Models." *Psychometrika* 64: 37–52.

Scheines, R., P. Spirtes, C. Glymour, and C. Meek (1994). *TETRAD II*. Hillsdale, N.J.: Lawrence Erlbaum.

Schulz, L. (2001). "On Again, Off Again: Causal Reasoning in Preschool Children." Poster, Society for Research in Child Development.

Shallice, T. (1988). *From Neuropsychology to Mental Structure*. Cambridge: Cambridge University Press.

Sheps, M. (1958). "Shall We Count the Living or the Dead?" *New England Journal of Medicine* 259: 1210–1214.

Schervish, Mark, T. Seidenfeld, and J. Kadane (forthcoming). "How Sets of Coherent Probabilities May Serve as Models for Degrees of Incoherence." *Journal of Uncertainty, Fuzziness, and Knowledge-Based Systems*.

Shipley, B. (1995). "Structured Interspecific Determinants of Specific Leaf Area in 34 Species of Herbaceous Angiosperms." *Functional Ecology* 9: 312–319.

Shipley, B. (1997). "Exploratory Path Analysis with Applications in Ecology and Evolution." *American Naturalist* 149: 1113–1138.

Shipley, B. (1999). "Exploring Hypothesis Space: Examples from Organismal Biology." In C. Glymour and G. Cooper, eds., *Computation, Causation and Discovery*. Cambridge: MIT Press.

Shipley, B. (2000). *Cause and Correlation in Biology*. Oxford: Oxford University Press.

Spearman, Charles (1904). "General Intelligence Objectively Determined and Measured." *American Journal of Psychology* 10: 151–293.

Spellman, B. A. (1996a). "Acting as Intuitive Scientists: Contingency Judgments Are Made While Controlling for Alternative Potential Causes." *Psychological Science* 7: 337–342.

Spellman, B. A. (1996b). "Conditionalizing Causality." In D. R. Shanks, K. J. Holyoak, and D. L. Medin, eds., *Causal Learning*, The Psychology of Learning and Motivation, no. 34. San Diego: Academic Press.

Spirtes, P. (1993). "Directed Cyclic Graphs, Conditional Independence, and Non-recursive Linear Structural Equation Models." Technical report CMU-Phil-35, Department of Philosophy, Carnegie Mellon University.

Spirtes, P. (1995). "Directed Cyclic Graphical Representations of Feedback Models." In *Proceedings of the 1995 Conference on Uncertainty in Artificial Intelligence, Montreal*, pp. 491–498. San Francisco, Calif.: Morgan Kaufman.

Spirtes, P. (1996). "Discovering Causal Relations among Latent Variables in Directed Acyclic Graphical Models." Technical report, CMU-Phil-69, Department of Philosophy, Carnegie Mellon University.

Spirtes, P., C. Glymour, and R. Scheines (1990). "Causality from Probability." J. E. Tiles, G. T. McKee, and G. C. Dean, eds., *Evolving Knowledge in Natural Science and Artificial Intelligence*. London: Pitman.

Spirtes, P., C. Glymour, and R. Scheines (1993, 2000). *Causation, Prediction, and Search*. Springer Lecture Notes in Statistics. 2nd revised edition. Cambridge: MIT Press.

Spirtes, P., C. Meek, and T. Richardson (1996). "Causal Inference in the Presence of Latent Variables and Selection Bias." In P. Besnard and S. Hanks, eds., *Proceedings of the Eleventh Conference on Uncertainty in Artificial Intelligence*, pp. 499–506. San Francisco: Morgan Kaufmann Publishers.

Stigler, S. (1986). *The History of Statistics*. Cambridge: Harvard University Press.

Suppes, P., and M. Zanotti (1981). "When Are Probabilistic Explanations Possible?" *Synthese* 48: 191–199.

Taubes, G. (1993). *Bad Science: The Short Life and Weird Times of Cold Fusion*. New York: Random House.

Thomson, G. (1939). *The Factorial Analysis of Human Ability*. Boston: Houghton Mifflin.

Thurstone, L. (1935). *The Vectors of Mind*. Chicago: University of Chicago Press.

Thurstone, L. (1947). *Multiple-Factor Analysis: A Development and Expansion of the Vectors of Mind*. Chicago: University of Chicago Press.

Van Hamme, Linda J., and Edward A. Wasserman (1994). "Cue Competition in Causality Judgements: The Role of Nonpresentation of Compound Stimulus Elements." *Learning and Motivation* 25: 127–151.

Watson, John (1972). "Smiling, Cooing, and 'the Game'." *Mirrill-Palmer Quarterly* 18: 323–339.

Watson, John (1979). "Perception of Contingency as a Determinant of Social Responsiveness." In E. B. Thoman, ed., *The Origins of Social Responsiveness*, pp. 33–64. New York: Erlbaum.

Watson, John, and C. Ramey (1972). "Reactions to Response Contingent Stimulation in Early Infancy." *Merrill-Palmer Quarterly* 18: 219–227.

Zurif, E., D. Swinney, and J. Fodor (1990). "An Evaluation of Assumptions underlying the Single-Patient-Only Position in Neuropsychological Research: A Reply." Preprint, Division of Linguistics and Cognitive Science, Brandeis University.

Index